W9-BRK-380

LEARNING TO TEACH
IN URBAN SCHOOLS

LEARNING TO TEACH
IN URBAN SCHOOLS

DOROTHY M. McGEOCH

with

CAROL R. BLOOMGARDEN

ELLEN O. FUREDI

LYNNE W. RANDOLPH

EUGENE D. RUTH, Jr.

LC5131
.M14L

66928

LC5131.M14L ST. JOSEPH'S UNIVERSITY STX
Learning to teach in urban schools

RELEASE

3 9353 00040 0075

TEACHERS COLLEGE PRESS

Teachers College, Columbia University

New York · 1965

Copyright ©1965 by Teachers College, Columbia University
Library of Congress Catalog Card Number: 65-22440
Manufactured in the United States of America

Cover design by Laurance T. Randolph

Introduction

This is a book about first-year teachers in the slum schools of a great city system. It is the story of four individuals who chose to work with children of the inner city and of their experiences in carrying out their decisions.

The four teachers were different in many respects. Their cultural backgrounds were quite dissimilar and they grew up and attended school and college in widely separated parts of the country. Only one decided early in life that he wanted to teach; two spent several years in other work.

They are alike in some ways, however. All have in common a stable and happy family life with many cultural and educational advantages. In each household it was expected that the children would go to college, and this expectation was a part of family and individual planning. All graduated from liberal arts colleges with majors in an academic area and prepared for teaching in a fifth-year program in a graduate college of education.

During the first half of their year of professional preparation, the prospective teachers were assigned to selected schools in depressed urban areas. They spent two or three days a week in classroom activities and in becoming acquainted with the total school community. They participated in after-school recreation and club programs. They attended parents' meetings, teachers' meetings and inservice education conferences and became acquainted with many aspects of the life of the professional teacher.

Full-time student teaching came during the second semester of the program and the four student teachers volunteered for a special group which became known as the Teaching Corps. Through the cooperation of the public school system, the college and community agencies, which provided special resources and financial support, the Teaching Corps participated in a program which included four related aspects: student teaching in an urban school in a depressed area, weekly seminars for cooperating teachers from the schools, a coordinated series of community experiences and sessions with resource personnel and special seminars and evaluation sessions during and at the end of the experience.

The schools which were chosen to participate in the project serve an area of housing projects and crumbling tenements, of poverty and loneliness and broken homes, of racial tension and a frighteningly high rate of delinquency. But it is also an area where many capable and active school people are working hard against great odds in the schools, where strong and well-established community agencies cooperate to deal with common problems, and where governmental agencies are working with private foundations in a coordinated attack on the causes of poverty and unemployment.

After one semester in this community as student teachers, the four members of the group returned as regular teachers to continue their work with disadvantaged children in the elementary schools. During their first year they met each week to discuss their experiences as teachers, the problems they encountered, and the insights they developed. As the coordinator of their preservice program, I met with them and recorded all the discussion sessions. I also visited their classrooms, talked with principals, and conferred individually with each of the beginning teachers at frequent intervals.

As time went on, we became increasingly convinced that other new teachers or prospective teachers might be helped by an account of our experiences. Extensive interviews with each teacher were then recorded. Background information and more detailed accounts of each teacher's feelings about himself and his teaching were obtained. Further group recordings focused on curriculum problems, special class activities, and projected plans for the following year.

Each teacher's story is told in his own words. Typescripts of the individual interviews, the seminar meetings and group discussions have been used as have written records and reports prepared at various times during the two years. From this truly formidable mass of material, coherent professional histories have been developed. That much that is personal slips in is not surprising since the teacher is first of all an individual person with his own way of looking at his work and his world.

Ellen, Lynne, Carol, and Gene each faced a different situation and responded in his or her own way. Their problems and their programs were different. An attempt has been made to preserve these differences while disguising certain incidents and comments to prevent embarrassment to others involved. In some cases, experiences of one member of the group have been attributed to another for the sake of further disguising the identity of individuals but, in general, the experiences are told as they were perceived by each participant.

This book is concerned with informing and assisting the beginning teacher in depressed urban areas. We realize, however, that what we have said here has many implications for administrators and teacher educators. The activities described suggest that the initial teaching experience of even the best prepared teachers is focused largely on learning to organize a classroom, to deal with behavior problems and to overcome the fear of losing control. Survival may be promoted by supervisory assistance, by sympathetic guidance, and by provisions for group support and discussion. But some degree of security must be achieved before substantial curriculum modifications can be made. It may well be that the growth of a competent teacher in these circumstances occurs in two overlapping stages: first, survival, and second, curriculum development. The experience of these teachers would seem to give support to such a hypothesis.

Perhaps more than anything else this book reveals how

little is known about effective ways of teaching in depressed urban areas. It may be that its greatest contribution is in making clear the difficulties and problems which prevail. But the four teachers have only begun to learn. Each has returned to his school for a second year and is continuing his battle for understanding and skill. With the recruitment of increasing numbers of young teachers like these, new insights may be reflected in better programs, commitment and dedication given support and encouragement, and intelligent effort rewarded by some evidence of success.

If we may in some slight degree contribute to this hoped-for outcome, all our struggles will not have been without result.

DMM

Acknowledgments

Many groups and individuals contributed significantly to the learning of the teachers whose experiences are recounted here. To all of them and especially to Mr. John C. Copp, college supervisor; to the cooperating teachers and the teacher-training coordinator of the schools which participated in the student teaching program; and to the district officers, administrators, teachers, and pupils of the schools where the four teachers are presently employed, go heartfelt thanks and appreciation. The transcription of many, many hours of recorded interviews and seminar sessions was made possible through a grant from the Faculty Research Fund at Teachers College. For support and encouragement throughout the project, we are greatly indebted to Dr. A. Harry Passow and Dr. Abraham Tannenbaum.

Contents

1

Prologue

Teaching in slum schools is hard work. Children who have learned to distrust adults, to expect failure in school, and to settle most problems with their fists are not easy to handle. Many schools are old and crowded; classes are often large; supplies and materials are inadequate or inappropriate. Some staff members are openly waiting for transfers or are past caring for anything but their monthly paycheck. For the conscientious and competent educator, the undiscriminating community dissatisfaction with the inadequacies of the segregated urban school can be frustrating and disheartening. Little support and less recognition is the lot of the typical teacher in such a school.

Then why should any young teacher choose such a situation or serve if he is assigned to a slum school? For precisely the reasons that hard and discouraging and necessary tasks have always had a fascination for the strong and the resolute —the need, the urge to overcome, the keenly felt but reluctantly verbalized convictions which motivate Peace Corps volunteers and Civil Rights workers—all of these lead to service as teachers in situations which provide the greatest difficulty and present the greatest challenge.

Let us make no mistake—not every young person with high purposes and a desire to serve will make a successful and satisfied teacher of disadvantaged children. Starry-eyed idealism and unrealistic aspirations can be as defeating as uncertainty and rejection. It takes solid purpose, extensive preparation, dogged persistence, and a pioneering spirit to

1

teach in a slum school. A touch of toughness tempered with unfailing compassion; a bent for organization combined with essential flexibility; a respect for high standards and a recognition of realistic limitations; a flair for innovation and creativity with a tolerance for unavoidable restrictions and limitations; a far-reaching purpose supported by a willingness to proceed, difficult step by difficult step, toward partial realization—these are the characteristics of the teachers who chose to teach, and to remain, in the schools of the urban core.

But how is an ordinary human being with a desire to make a contribution to society to assess his own potential and interest in this area of service? Only experience in the schools over a period of time can finally answer this question. However, the prospective teacher's reaction to the professional histories presented in this volume may be one clue to his possible interest. If he identifies with one or more of the beginning teachers, if the problems they face present a personal challenge, if the rewards they find seem important, if their experiences are neither distasteful nor unduly discouraging; then perhaps further exploration and experience should be sought. These case histories will have served their purpose if they are useful both to the prospective teacher choosing a field of service and to the beginning teacher in surviving his first year.

2

"It's hardest at the beginning...

. . . when you aren't
sure of your own
authority. You aren't
quite ready to tangle
with all the problems.
Tremendously you want
this to be smooth and
peaceful and good. It
may take a year to
realize just how
much authority you
really have."

When I entered the preservice program I was considering teaching gifted children. Certainly the idea of working in a depressed-area school had never occurred to me. I knew very little about any kind of school and nothing about slum children. My thinking has changed a lot over the last two years.

All of us were assigned to schools in depressed areas for our first student-teaching experience. I was sent to a section of the city which was new to me, but which seemed to have strange connotations for friends of mine. It was supposedly rough, not particularly safe, and no place to be if you wanted pleasant working conditions and respectful, coooperative children.

Well, I've been there nearly two years now and I like it. My husband and I have bought a cooperative apartment very close to the school where I am teaching. I feel a genuine at-homeness with the community, with the people—adults and children—that makes me look forward to continuing to live and work there.

I admit that I did not come to this conclusion immediately. I grew into it through exposure. It was rather like meeting a person. First you hear a lot about him, you see him for the first time, you finally get to know what he is really like, and only then can you like him for what he is. Before that you have only hearsay or sight judgments to go by, and these are superficial, not fair. So, in a nutshell, it was through complete exposure, really getting acquainted with the community, that I came to feel a part of it.

I feel a part of the children; I know them, their spontaneity, enthusiasm, freedom, humor, innocence—all the childlike qualities that make them children. In these qualities, they are not deprived or disadvantaged. They are still children and can be reached as children. More important, they want to be reached and cared about and taught.

At first, of course, I was surprised. Surprised by appearance which was unlike that of children I knew. But they are children in spite of clothes that are not new, hair that is not always brushed, hands and necks that are often far from clean, language that is ungrammatical and frequently profane. All of this does not eliminate the child qualities that are there. I now know these children—Negro, Puerto Rican, and "others." I am no longer shocked by attitudes of rebellion, disappointment, indifference.

If I had not been prepared to meet this, I would be discouraged by it. I would not be able to recognize it as a learned response or a defense response instead of a characteristic of the child. I have been exposed to teachers and other people who explained to me and helped me to know how things in the child's life and experience induced these behaviors. I am more ready to deal with them as alien forces in the child's individuality, forces that can be modified through understanding teaching.

In my first semester, I shook hands with the South Bay area. I met teachers, children, and community people. I learned all the shocking information from people dealing with problems first hand. Teachers told anecdotes about children involved with glue sniffing, sex, stealing, and teacher baiting. I also saw some of these things for myself. Observing classrooms I saw teacher-controlled classes and child-controlled classes. I saw the difficulties of trying to teach there.

More than other things, however, it was the teacher attitudes that amazed me. I was stunned to hear teachers griping and indifferent and bored with their work. I really think these children have a right to teachers who like being with them. At least in school, they can learn fairness and unselfishness and kindness—but only if they have teachers expressing these qualities. I think they learn what they see more than what they are told.

At the same time, we often spoke with a teacher who was in charge of a particularly notorious class. This teacher is dedicated and sincere. He took members of his class home with him, went on trips after school, and spent time of his own with his children's problems. This teacher inspired me because he was doing what I was just beginning to feel. He was not glib. He knew the difficulties and was doing an excellent job, being a teacher in the real sense to his children.

As part of our program I worked in a recreation center one afternoon a week, assisting in a ceramics class. I learned much through this experience, for I saw children expressing themselves there as they could not always do in the classroom. As they pounded out their feelings on the clay in front of them, I sensed the need for attention, for making something of their own, for success. Witnessing children working with clay at the recreation center showed me vividly how much art can do to relieve them and give them satisfaction.

Our group of student teachers made a film during that first semester. All of the seminar groups were studying their communities and many of them were taking pictures. We wanted to do something that no one had done. Filming was a step beyond photography, we thought. It was fun to do.

The film also made us get out, walk around, and see things in a more particular light. We looked at the streets for something that was interesting and colorful. I remember all of us and our college supervisor in front of the school at seven-thirty in the morning to get shots of the flag raising at the housing projects. As we focused our camera on faces and buildings, feet and streets, my own perspective altered. It sharpened my own vision and I saw more clearly the people—their moods, ages, identities became more apparent. They emerged from the general community we were studying as individuals, with distinct identity and interest.

Once we heard a youngster remark, "Look at them—takin' pictures of the poor people." We felt terrible, for we were no longer outsiders taking inside pictures. We were already looking with an insider's eye. After all, didn't we teach in the school on the corner? Through this self-conscious remark we learned a little more about the slum dwellers as people with feeling and dignity, not to be invaded or inspected for general consumption.

Well, after awhile you begin to know someone well enough and to like him a lot. After that film, we liked the neighborhood. Some of the people we felt closest to were the members of the Parents Association. These mothers, once they realized we were student teachers, really welcomed us. In one taped interview they told us all about their hopes for their children and their concern for the school. They, too, were aware of the indifference of some of the members of the community. They understood, better than we, the family problems that interfered with parent participation in school activities. As they saw their role in school affairs, they could help in getting other parents to take an interest in school. They talked about classes for the gifted, about class mothers, about selling coffee in the hall for teachers, and about problems at home. It was not hard for us to talk to each other for we had the children, the school, and the community in common.

That was all during the first semester. The college then asked if some of us would care to continue in our schools for the second semester of student teaching. The prospect of being in a pilot group challenged me. It meant an opportunity to participate in an exciting project that was dealing with urban school problems. This feeling of being a special group, of having our opinions and reactions considered where it meant something, was an inducement. This challenge and appeal to our intelligence was attractive to all of us.

So, besides normal student teaching, we sat in on conferences and lectures sponsored by community agencies and gained insight into the behavior and background of the children. We heard some specialists speak and some specialists listened to us. It was new, exciting, and encouraging.

At school we had great support. It was as if we were in class all day. I was watching a master teacher whose skill both encouraged and discouraged me. I saw an example of teaching that I tried to reach. Certainly this class proved to me that the children were most teachable, new approaches could be tried, classes could be interested and alert. It was important that I see class and teacher operating so successfully together. This proved that it could be done and this was what I needed to be sure of.

But I really didn't have a very good time in student teaching. I was in a class, the class with the highest ability on the grade level, and I really didn't have control when the teacher was out of the room. I couldn't walk down the stairs with them alone. They knew I was vulnerable. I would end up crying, and they laughed.

I didn't feel that I was improving at all. It was a very dejected feeling. I was not as capable as I wanted to be. I would be nervous coming to school in the morning. That's why I started out tough in my own classroom, which I think stood me in good stead. It's been much easier this year. I've been captain of my own ship and I just love it. It's been the difference between day and night.

My cooperating teacher commanded absolute respect and obedience, and she did a lot of teaching. She was concerned about many things. If a child picked up a pencil while I was teaching, I was supposed to see him and make him put it down. So I was looking for all the little things and when I stopped for them of course I couldn't hold the attention of the class, and I lost out on what I was trying to do. It wasn't so much that I didn't want to be second in authority, but I just didn't feel—well, partly it was the control. It was a combination of all those things but the complete joy—having a good time teaching, which makes it heaven for you and the children—just wasn't there.

It wasn't until the very end, when our seminar group sat down with the books that we had read and tried to think of conclusions for our report, that things began to come into focus. It was those last weeks that we spent in a room by ourselves that brought everything together. Before then I don't think I was so inspired about children who needed this special teaching in order to learn. In student teaching I just didn't feel that the teacher was doing anything extra because she did it so smoothly. But during those two weeks, as I remember it now, I began to understand what teaching was all about.

I have come a long way since I left college and came to the big city for a job. I had been a government major and had already decided to work for a nonprofit organization that was doing some world service. I got a telephone book, went down the list of those organizations, and found employment with the Council on Foreign Relations, working in their library.

I was an only child and perhaps I grew up faster because we moved all over. I was forced to go from one group into another, to make friends with strangers. Once we counted the elementary schools I had gone to, and there were ten or eleven. It just made me rely more on myself. I think I found out what I was about earlier than I would have otherwise.

I remember that every few years my father would come home and announce that he was being transferred. So I grew to expect that, periodically, we would be moving and I would look forward to it. It was kind of a happy thing because we would move to a new house, which was exciting, and I would go to a new school. It was sad sometimes, leaving my friends, but it wasn't a horrible thing.

When I was in the eighth grade I got to help the second grade teacher. I was the school monitor and I was stationed outside her door. I loved Miss Jones so much I think I probably offered to help her. The big treat was writing on the blackboard. She would let me put questions on the board. That was very exciting. But I know I never wanted to be a teacher, because nine to three seemed so long.

There was never any question about college though, I always knew I would go. I applied to only one college and went there. It was a very unique place. I don't talk about it to people who haven't been there as I am sure it would be a hard thing to communicate without sounding like something that I'm really not. There was a fantastic sense of friendliness and closeness. It was a church-related school and, of course, your religion is very important to you. It is probably one of the strongest ties you have if you take it seriously. So it generates a strength from within that does more things than any artificial masthead or slogan.

At school I had my introduction to world affairs. I had not thought on a world-wide base at all. It was my introduction to people from all parts of the world. That is why I majored in government which is something that is very important to me. And the languages! I loved languages! I spent two years with German and two years with Spanish.

I went to Germany for a summer and got a job working among German-speaking people only. This was a good way to learn the language. I lived on the fifth floor of one of those old houses that was cut up, on the side of Alster Bay, a beautiful, beautiful spot in the old section of Hamburg. I worked for my father's company and knew the man who headed the office. They lived next door, so I had a bath once in a while—they had warm water and I didn't.

The next summer I went to the University of Mexico with a group from school and studied Spanish. I think I developed deeper ties with other countries than if I hadn't had the languages.

I wasn't very conscious of the poor people in Mexico. I have just finished reading *The Children of Sanchez,* and over and over I thought, where were they when I was in Mexico? They were not pointed out. It just shows how much my thinking has changed—how far my interests have gone away from myself.

I didn't plan to get married. I left all that behind when I decided that I wanted to work and have a career and really do something. I have a thing about women getting out and contributing a little bit instead of just having babies. This is something that I am positively serious about. I think that women can fill a much bigger role than they are used to—or are used to wanting. Getting married was something that just happened. I was in love and he asked me and so I got married.

I always feel that I must have my own reasons. Even now what I do must be *my* reason for doing it—not anyone else's. I feel that it is safer that way, more balanced. Sometimes if you are counting on a person—or on a thing—it isn't as safe as if you make up your mind for yourself.

After we were married I found work in the library of the Council on Foreign Relations. My job, with a B.A., was to type up library catalog cards for books and I did it just as long as I could stand it. I tried to think up everything else I could do on that job and yet my job was typing up catalog cards and unless I wanted to be a librarian there was nothing else I could do. It was a very limiting job but it did show me office work for what it was. I saw secretaries who had been there a long time with more responsible jobs. They were typing up letters for men. It seemed there was very little creative that they could do. They were limited.

So then I knew I had to go to school. I thought of getting a master's degree in international relations, but I wasn't very excited about taking more government courses. It just didn't seem to be what I wanted to do. I don't know just what happened, but I knew I wanted to do something where I could do some thinking—probably in the area of service, too. So teaching seemed to fit into those categories.

I made an appointment for an interview with the coordinator of a fifth-year program in elementary education. She didn't seem to think that I had enough experience with children and sent me out to visit some schools. I went but I wasn't interested. I was bored watching the whole thing go on and there didn't seem much that encouraged me. I didn't stay very long because the children were reading on their own, and it didn't seem like anything was going on. I'm sure I'd see much more today, just looking at the room. But I didn't then. In fact, I ended up seeing a junior high school and talking about English.

I did go to talk to someone about preparing to teach English in high school. The man just said that if I liked to correct a lot of papers I should do it. I think he must have had to correct a lot himself. If he had been more enthusiastic, I might have considered it. I really didn't have enough English credits anyway and would have had to take a lot of undergraduate English courses plus the courses for a master's degree in English. It would have been quite a long haul. With a liberal arts degree, the elementary school program was just perfect for me.

Up until March of that year I had never thought of teaching. Then it entered my mind, and I started taking steps. The more I thought about the idea, the more acceptable it seemed, and the more enthusiastic I got. I had to write a statement about what I thought about teaching when I applied. It doesn't seem that I wrote it a long time ago at all. It's very familiar.

I wrote, "I've thought very carefully about being a teacher. After graduating from college I looked for work which was providing a service for mankind. Office work in a service organization did not enable me to make the individual contribution that I had hoped to make. I want work that is

satisfying and creative and demanding. That last word, I
think, is more important to me than the other two. Teaching
embodies all of that. My goal is to be a good teacher. To meet
with receptivity and give it real nourishment. I would want
to awaken, to make aware, to arouse appreciation of quality
in the class that I would teach. I want to inspire young people
to want quality. A good teacher does all of this through her
love of children and her example as a grown-up. I would not
want to be less than a good teacher."

I'm sure that I knew that statement might have an effect
on my getting into the program, but I had been writing similar things on a lot of resumes, not just the teacher one. I
guess then I wanted to do a good job at something more than
I really wanted to be a teacher.

I can see that, over the last two years, my concept of
teaching has been expanding. In the beginning all the girls
I knew who didn't really want to put forth an effort went into
teaching. All the girls who were going to have babies in two
years were teachers. All the girls I knew who didn't think or
read very much were teachers. I had a concept of the person
of a teacher that held me off. Then I started liking the idea
of the job—little by little—and I started working in the preservice program. A new aspect opened up—working with the
underprivileged child—which was more interesting because
it was more challenging. Really, if this gets easy I wouldn't
want to do it!

I'm glad I'm not having to start all over again, though.
All last summer I dreaded it. I was to be in a different school
that I knew nothing about. I looked forward to teaching with
fear and trembling. I wouldn't think about it, and as it got
closer and closer it was like Doomsday. I was really very
scared of it all, but it was much smoother than I expected. I
had anticipated all kinds of things going wrong, children not
doing what I told them, and complete chaos.

But I found out the first day, of course, that they were
ready to come to school, that they were on their best behavior,
and this gave me the confidence that I needed. Every day I
would ride the bus with my heart right up in my throat and I
would plunge in and it would be lunchtime and it would be

over and it would be all right. Two more hours and we would get through and getting through was the big thing, just having them respond and get used to me.

My group is the fourth level of the sixth grade. The children are not able to do independent work like the class I had in the other school when I was student teaching. The assignments are much different because they cannot read independently. I thought the difference was much bigger in the beginning but it isn't so big to me now, because I realize that the other sixth-grade class was desperately in need of background and so is my class. I couldn't take too much for granted with that first class, even though they had the slight edge in reading skills.

I don't feel that the spirit of the room—the socializing— is so different either. In fact, I like it better in my own room. You might expect a kind of low morale feeling, but I don't think that is the case.

Reading has been the area in which there has been the most development. In the beginning it was so hard because I was trying to find a book that would appeal to them on their level, but a book that they hadn't met two or three grades before. All I could find was a battered set of fourth-grade books—covers off, pages missing—just the most unappealing set of books I have ever seen. I didn't even want to open them. There was no teacher's edition there either, and I needed one.

I opened the box and we started to pass them out, amid groans and groans and groans. Then I decided, no—we can't do this. So I put them away and that was the last we used them. Then I got the books from the college that saved me. They were fourth-grade books that the class had never seen before. I had sixteen of those, and we made a big deal about them.

I split my class up and gave half of them the new books and then I got a fifth-grade reader which looked very exciting. It is a beautifully done book—beautiful pictures and everything—and I passed it out to the other half. But we found, as we went along, that it was a very complicated book —all about engines and trains. It didn't even seem real to me. It was trying to tell them stories, but there was so much

information that it was not doing either job—factual informing or fun reading. The girls started saying, "Oh no! Not
this again." And even the boys did not have the knowledge to
know the parts or even want to look at the pictures, or anything. It was hard to motivate them—hard to make them
interested.

So I got rid of that book and got another fifth-grade
book, which is also very hard for them. It's beautiful; I like
it better than the other one. The stories are about other lands
and are just the sort of thing these children like.

When I first tried to break the class down into two
groups, I was so afraid that, when I was working with one
group, the other wouldn't be able to work alone. That was
exactly the way it was for a long time, but I kept at it and
we're just beginning to have the two groups working well.
I put the assignment on the board for the group working
alone. I explain it and make sure that they understand it and
they work on their own. I put one child in charge, and only
that child is allowed to interrupt me when I'm working with
the other group. This happens when there is something they
really don't understand. I'm very proud of them. I frequently congratulate them because I can trust them to work
alone.

Sometimes I split up the group I am with and work with
about eight children at the back table while the others are
reading at their seats. It seems that the smaller the group
the better able I am to know what they have really read.
Otherwise, they can just sit there and fool me. Often, they
understand a little bit but they really don't understand all the
concepts in the story.

We go over the stories page by page, and I ask, "What
does this word mean?" or "Let's think of another word for
it." I don't know if it is right but they love to work in small
groups, and I couldn't do this with the whole class. I have
been trying to give the class an independent activity—math
or another subject—in the afternoon; then I can work with
the small groups. I use the SRA materials with groups, too.
The SRA program is wonderful but it doesn't take the place
of my basal reader. I have to work with them to strengthen
comprehension and build their vocabulary.

I have had a hard time trying to learn to do group work because in the beginning I wanted them to work like a little army of soldiers—pick up their pencils at the same time and put them down together. I hated interruptions. At first, I wasn't able to distinguish among interruptions that were important, interruptions that were unnecessary, and interruptions that were just disorderly. I was so frantically trying to hold my class together that it didn't make any difference whether it was the principal, a child with a message, or the janitor who came in—it was just an interruption that made me take my eyes off the class.

This is not as silly as it sounds, because I do think it is important for the children to learn to do things together the right way; routines must be established, but, of course, I carried it too far. The assumption was that they could all do it the same way—not only the routine but also the school-work—and that's not true.

Also, I wasn't sure of them; I didn't know them, and I didn't know what to expect in my own classroom or what I wanted them to do. There was always the off chance that they would run away or that someone would become too hard to handle and it would tear down the morale of the whole class. After I got to know them, I could take each incident in a kind of perspective and say, "Well, he's doing it because of . . . ." or "This is all right. This can go on while we're doing something else." At the beginning I didn't have any norms to compare anything with. Another teacher's class isn't your norm. Another teacher's class doesn't have anything to do with you. You just have to establish what is good and what is not good and what you want or can tolerate.

The very first day, Richard refused to have his name card on his desk. I'm glad I didn't know his background, because it would have scared me to death. He had already been transferred out of one school. He had been in two classes the previous year, and, later, one of the teachers told me that he was "hell on wheels." Anyway, he refused to take his name card.

I was so anxious to have everything right that I was bending over backwards for each particular child (something I don't do now, but I could do more). Everyone seemed a potential problem. I was so aware of the differences of these children and their special needs, that I wanted to help them—I would do anything to help them.

There were signs that Richard was different, but I just ignored him and went on. He didn't do much that day but he continued to be the one I had to watch the most. I gave him more attention than anyone else. Recently, I haven't been so bothered by him, but he has been truant more often. I am not as afraid of him—he is not the threat that he was—so I haven't done as much for him. This hasn't been good, either, because he needs someone to give him just as much attention as I did at the beginning. It's not fair to neglect the other children but I can see that, if I'm not careful, he'll drop out of school. When he comes back after being truant it's not the same. He is a little further away, a little less interested and less anxious to be good.

I have to watch Sammy, too. I can't keep up with that boy. He is so active, so alive, and so intelligent that he could run away to the library and I probably wouldn't know it. He is just always doing something a little bit different. He whizzes through his work so quickly that just to keep him going I need about a ten-year project for him.

Then there is Santos, who does his work all right but is the kind of boy who is always out of his seat, always raising his hand right in front of my face with some question or other. But, outside of those three or four characters, the rest of them do pretty much what is expected of them.

I am able to do more now; but, where I used to be afraid, now it is annoyance rather than worry about a particular child. I'm not on tenterhooks now, so I'm better able to convince a disorderly child that he better snap into line and stop ruining everything. This shows my impatience, which I don't like either, but I do believe that things have to be orderly or the children are not going to learn.

This doesn't mean there can't still be a lot of group work and a lot of good project work, but the room has to be quiet for learning; each child should know what he is to do, know the limits of the room, and be in his place. As soon as somebody calls out or yells across the room, it is distracting. I don't mind when they whisper or talk quietly about what they have to do, but even that should be kept to a minimum.

I have a conscious feeling of security, sometimes, standing up there, knowing that if this problem had come up a few weeks earlier, I would be dying. But I know and they know that this isn't so serious, and we'll go ahead. I remember just after Christmas feeling a great relief that I didn't have to be quite as disturbed about little things as I had been before. There is tremendous pressure, and you are never without some problem.

I am learning to take pressure better than I did. They really do push you. All the hands waving! If someone misses something they are right there with the right answer before he has time to think. If someone stumbles over a word in reading they shout it out. When I get pushed near the panic point, I tend to go faster and faster. I want to scream all over the place. But if I can only get very quiet and look around and say slowly, "All right. That will do for now," it's like play-acting, and they laugh and quiet down.

The best thing, the most satisfying thing of all, is when they are all working. When they're sitting there all involved, each one working at his own rate, I feel there is that—not exactly organization—but rhythm to the room. I just feel good because I can be working somewhere in the corner and I can just feel that sort of hum. It is a good hum, not foolish. It doesn't happen too often, but it's the best thing—even better than their being excited because then they always have to settle down again and get back to work. Often during art class, which they all like, they will really get down to work.

I want to do much more with art next year. I like it. Again there has been this pressure to read and write and learn. I haven't even set up the easel I made because I've lost a screw. Now that kind of thing is just too silly. You can get clogged up in the littlest, most miniscule details; and they will hold you completely immobile. It's like getting so far in arithmetic and realizing there is a mental block with you and with the children, and nobody is getting it. And then hating to go back to it because it is so hard to break through. I don't even want to talk about math because I'm so rotten.

We've gotten stymied on so many avenues. We go for a certain length of time and establish some basic understanding; then half the class gets behind and I don't exactly know how to cope with the situation. One group knows this much, and the other group isn't able to do anything. So I drop it and we begin something else. Fractions we went into . . . . We got the most elemental things and then reached the point where some of them were able to go on but most of them weren't—so we dropped it. Now we are on measures and the same thing is happening.

I think math is one of the hardest subjects to teach. It sounds easy to do it by the discovery method. Boy, I'd like to put my college professor down in that class. You wait and you wait and you wait for a child to come up with the answer. You lose half the class and finally when he does figure it out, he has the wrong answer.

I think math through understanding, the way I was taught, is wonderful because it made me understand the way I never understood math before. I understand the way it's done but I haven't got it in my bones, so I can't teach that way. It's much harder with sixth graders. Arithmetic is something that they have learned, not something they have tried to understand. They learned what to do. They did it and they tried to do it correctly. Even my best students did this. It's much harder than it would be if I was just trying to build on the rote work that they know.

I am learning, too, with them, learning the way they are learning. I have to unlearn everything and I find myself all of a sudden stopped. I throw up my hands and go back to, "We'll finish this problem the way I learned it and the way you learned it." Later I can sit down and figure out how it ought to be done.

I want to do much more next year. We should do more rigorous learning, establishing basic concepts of what things mean. There is just so much of the thinking of arithmetic— mathematical thinking—that they don't realize and we take for granted that they learned in kindergarten. Then it comes to story problems. How do we get the answer? And they come up with every process but division. They don't see any relationships or why they do anything. It's like starting all over again.

I haven' t done so well with science either. I haven't seemed to be able to find too many things that they were interested in. We haven't covered many units. We did something on the weather but it was kind of hop-skip-jump.

Every science experiment I have ever done has failed. I don't know what happens. I can't count on the simplest thing to come off right. Usually, I perform the experiment, and they come up and taste something or hold it. Once I cut up a dry cell and two boys demonstrated the parts. It seems hard. I haven't been able to get the whole class involved.

We had a science coordinator come in—a wonderful man. His approach was so natural. He said it is not the facts they learn from reading the book, but what they are able to do about what they learn. He said that they probably know more about science than I do, which is true, and I should just help them to find out things for themselves. A lot of my boys do read science books in their free time.

About half my children have library cards. In the beginning I said everyone had to have a card, but then I got notes from home: they hadn't returned their books; the library was very unjust; they paid a huge fine. So I just tried to supply everyone with a book from the school library.

We have a library table at the back of the room. Some of them will just look at magazines. It is important to point out the right book to the one who might be interested. If a child says, "I've read them all," or "There isn't anything I like," I'll say, "Let's go back and look." Usually he will find one he'll at least try, and maybe he will like it. It is not a phenomenal success, but most are doing some reading.

I do read to them though. I have been reading *Charlotte's Web*. I started *Wind in the Willows*—no good. I read some of *Tom Sawyer*. That was all right, but not wonderful, though. There was a lot of description and not enough narrative in some parts. Just getting them to be comfortable with books at all is the biggest problem. Just lately, however, the most wonderful thing has happened to us. Since the school library is across the hall, I am acquainted with the librarian, and she is now allowing our whole class to go in once a week.

We went there the other afternoon and spent the whole afternoon on committee work. It is a huge library; each group had a table, and each table had a topic of its own. The chairman got the books and took them to the table and each person found out just one interesting thing about the topic his group had. Then we had a quick time for reporting. It was such a good working way to learn this, it wasn't remote or removed.

The change from our room to the library and the extra space is good, too. They know that they are supposed to be quiet in the library, and they don't forget like they do in our room. I just love it; I want this same classroom next year, because we are so close to the library.

I'm very excited about next year. We are getting some literature books that will be fun and the most beautiful set of social studies books. This publisher has a whole series on foreign countries and South American countries. The funniest thing happened when I wrote to the publisher ordering sample texts. I said our school had some additional funds, and could they just send me samples. They sent them, but they billed me for ten books. They were addressed to "Mrs. Redford, Principal." I thought that I would have to return them, but our assistant principal was very understanding, and he said the school could pay for them.

They are the most beautiful books. I am going to put them on display somewhere. They have lots of pictures, mostly photographs. They give a real feeling of each country but are very easy reading. In fact, that is the purpose of these books but I've never seen them used in school, certainly not as textbooks. The publisher states that several grades could use these books. If each class had a set for a different country, they could be interchanged; it would be such an efficient use of textbooks.

I ordered all the same, Mexico, But I don't know how smart that was. I'm beginning to see that I could use different textbooks; I could divide them and say, "You look for this" and "You look for that" and "Let's compare." I could work on many skills in using different books. But I didn't think of that.

We are doing a play for assembly. We have costumes, the school has a whole bunch of costumes. They love to get dressed up and this is a good chance. Everybody is involved. They are very excited; they keep waiting and waiting and asking me every day when we are going to practice the play?

At the beginning of the year we tried a play in connection with social studies. After we knew all about Cortez and the people he was with, we did a play by ourselves, but I didn't think it was finished enough to put on in front of everyone.

One of the little girls brought in a book of plays, very short, very elementary, so I Rexographed several of them, and we did them different times, using different casts. The plays were so short and easy to learn that after the second time the children weren't using their scripts. They did them so well that I sent them into the room next door to do them for Miss Farlow's class. They were so pleased! I could have a student director and just sit there and watch them. We even had some original plays written by volunteers. There were some that were very, very good.

I think next year we could do a series of plays. It might be interesting to do them throughout the year—some printed and some original ones. Then we would have them all ready for assembly whenever our time came.

I am really happy with the writing we have been doing. Writing seems to have been the most spontaneous, the most happy thing we have done. We all get really whipped up over an idea together; we discuss it, and, since everybody can't talk at once, we have to write our ideas. They know just about the time we have to turn off the discussion, and they get their pencils out. We've done creative writing about things like going up in a balloon. That's one thing they liked. Then we all went to a restaurant together and wrote about what we had to eat.

In the beginning they would do just a minimum of writing and I didn't know how to ask them to do more, how to help them to see that they could do better. At first, they'd write a story, I'd look at it and give it back to them, they would do just the minimum corrections, and that was all. Now we are getting a little bit better, little bit deeper. I can say, "This isn't complete enough. You know what you can do and this isn't your best." They are beginning to pull a little bit more out of their own minds. I can see it happening, and it's very satisfying.

I have been thinking about a class magazine. I have saved their writing from the beginning of the year and I have found three parents with typewriters who can help. They are very excited about the idea.

I don't want to get involved in too many projects because we already have the play and we are going to do eight dances for the Park Fete. This includes the children from forty-four schools. Each sends two classes to the park one warm day in June; there is a children's band, and all the school officials are there. It's really supposed to be a big deal. We'll be practicing daily. I look forward to it and they do, too. It solves my gym problem.

We haven't gone to the gym much this year, although we are supposed to have two periods a week. The class is much harder to control there. I don't feel as sure in the gym. I haven't really spent much time learning games and getting the routine set up. I feel very guilty about it. Our gym supervisor has been with us twice. She's wonderful. She got us all organized as to how to stand on spots and dots and everything. I did it once with them but things came up, and I did not always make myself go—which was a mistake. I know I should get down there. This is one of the areas in which I have done a lousy job.

I like the dancing periods, and most of the children like them, too. I like dancing so much that I want them to do very well. I have very high standards, and I want things to happen too quickly.

There is one dear, tiny little boy who offered to run the record player for dancing. I had four couples ready to go and I was kind of on my tiptoes dancing around. I signaled that I was ready for the music, but he couldn't get the needle on the thread and we had to wait. I was worried about the record, I was worried that they'd get out of line. I literally swooped down like a vulture and said, "Never mind. Never mind. I'll do it." His face got red and he just shrank. He had offered to help me, but he wouldn't do it any more. I couldn't blame him; I'd scared him off. It was the most awful thing to do.

I had another bad thing happen during the dancing, too. I got in trouble with the assistant principal. It was really quite awful.

I had all the chairs pushed back and we were in dance position. We had established that people who dance will be the ones who want to, because they really have to pay attention for this. One of the boys started fooling around and bothering the others, so I sent him down to the office. The assistant principal sent him back. I just didn't have time to write a note so I sent him back again, hoping the assistant principal would recognize that this was an emergency situation. When the child came back again—I think it was the second or third time—I got the children in their seats and quiet, and then I went down with the child.

I explained to the assistant principal how hard it was, that I had them standing up all over the room, that I hadn't been close to pencil and paper. He wouldn't listen to me and he proceeded to be very adamant and unpleasant. So I said, "Well, you're right. I know I should send a note, and I certainly will from now on," and I left. Later I saw him in the office. I tried to explain and I said, "The only thing was I just needed help right then." He said it was all right, but the next time I must send a note with the child. All of this leaves the teacher feeling so much alone.

At the first of the year I had such a dismal, dreary kind of feeling. The whole school was ugly and rundown; the classes were nothing special. It seemed like a hard place to teach—no great new exciting experiments going on—it was just plodding with lots of poor teaching and lots of discouragement.

Now I understand better. I realize how hard it is and I know what the teachers are up against. Since I am up against the same things, I can sympathize more. Of course, I know them as people, too, and I like them as people, whereas they were just teachers before. Then, they either met my ideal or they fell. Now, they are friends, so I don't judge them quite as quickly.

I think there is potential in every school. I really think

more than ever that the administration has to take hold and demand the best from every teacher. If they would just say to one teacher who wasn't doing the job, "We can't have this in our school. You have to leave," it would make every teacher work harder. The administration can't do everything; it is the teachers really doing their jobs—their part of the hall or their part of the building or taking responsibility for making this the most orderly school that we can have.

Two things need to be done. First of all, chop off the dead wood and, then, the second thing, reward the good jobs that are being done. As in praising children, I think that to let the teacher know the job is really commendable, she is doing something fine, encourages that kind of work even if the teacher is already trying. And seeing the teacher who is not doing anything causes more chaos and tends to pull down the morale of everyone.

Maybe it could be done by just rewarding the positive because, of course, there is a lot more positive. I don't know whether you can go in and reward the good without doing anything about the poor, or whether it simply means that, when the good try to be better, the contrasts become more pronounced and the irritations, like kids running around the halls and knocking on doors, become greater. It's a hard question.

I still have a lot to learn in my own room. I began with the longest lessons you ever saw. I would have a math lesson and it would last an hour and a half. I don't think that is always wrong but you shouldn't consistently have hour and a half lessons. Now the lessons are much shorter; I think the variety in the morning session takes the place of some of the other kind of exercise that you might make room for. We do have milk, but it goes so smoothly that it is not an interruption. The children take care of it and collect the money so the class doesn't stop consciously for it.

In the beginning the milk was such a pain in the neck that we skipped it. If you don't send anybody down for milk, you don't have milk. First of all there was money to collect, and I kept forgetting the milk money. I had a list of Welfare children and non-Welfare children, but my kids kept telling me they were on Welfare. They all had to take slips home to have signed, but every time I sent the slips down to the office—there were about eighteen things to do—some names were scratched out. There was a great lack of communication between our room and the lunchroom. It was a huge rigamarole. It was just too much so we quit for awhile. Then we got two monitors who do a very good job, and everything has worked out very smoothly. They take care of it all with no trouble to anyone.

I tried another idea when I was learning how to set up routines. I would read to them and they were to listen quietly while they got their coats. We used that for maybe a week and a half and it worked but I didn't feel it was legitimate. They were more interested in getting their coats, of course, and they got involved in the routine of that rather than listening to what was read. A few listened, but not enough to make it really worthwhile. So I decided that, if we were going to have reading, it would be just for reading and not to keep them quiet while they got their coats.

It's hardest at the beginning, when you aren't sure of your own authority. You aren't quite ready to tangle with all the problems. Tremendously you want this to be smooth and peaceful and good. It may take a year to realize just how much authority you really have. I'm just beginning to feel that I really command the room, that I am the boss, that I want the child to do what I tell him to do and the reason is just because I tell him to do it.

I remember the first weeks when I was trying to get them in hand; it seemed such a gradual process, until finally we liked each other. It wasn't such a false thing when I was standing up there waiting for them to do what I said, hoping that they would do what I said. Finally, I understood that they would and they understood that they would. That was good.

But the great hurdles seemed to be: "How shall I teach this? What am I going to do in arithmetic? What should I assign for reading?" I made such a mish-mash of some subjects. I remember standing up there with some science lessons where I got way off the track. I don't know if I had not prepared enough or if they knew the answers that we were supposed to spend time discussing, but I would look at them and I would think, "Oh, you poor, poor children, you have such a green first-year teacher. How come you are being as good as you are?" Some would be misbehaving and I'd think, "Why don't more of you misbehave? How can you stand it?" I would be so far gone that I'd stand about a hundred feet from myself and think, "Let's change this. Get into something different or get out. What makes you think that you're a teacher anyway?"

But I really do like my class. Individual relationships are fine. There is an understanding and a freedom of talk and movement that I think is real growth. It is a result of our working together until we are really able to think together. This is evident from the remarks of other teachers who work with them. Mr. Pepper, the reading-improvement teacher, has often commented that he enjoys working with my class, that they are easy to work with, and that they respond to him. I think this must be, partly at least, a result of their feelings about what is going on in the classroom.

I hope that I'll have a class next year with some of the feeling that we have been able to develop this year—that good feeling that comes when we are all working hard and enjoying ourselves. I want the same grade level. I couldn't even begin to master the sixth-grade curriculum in one year. It will take at least three before I know it well enough to make any really important improvements, but I do hope to do a better job next year. I feel that I ought to want another low-achievement class, because that is what I was trained to teach. I should be using all the thought I put into this year. But I can't help wanting a more capable class, a class that I can do more with, a class more ready to be under control and better behaved at the beginning. So, I guess I really am hoping for a better class.

With a better class I wouldn't have to worry quite so much about this horrible problem of promotion to junior high school and all the mad testing that we have been having to get the reading level up so that they can pass.

The first standardized reading test was given in January, and about fifteen in my class failed to make the score that is required for promotion to junior high. So this group has been coached all spring by a special reading teacher in addition to the work we have done in the room.

They are being coached on how to take a reading examination. They are given small tests similar to the examination, and then they are retested. I think that the tests that are being given now are more adapted to an area like ours. At any rate, all but two or three have finally been able to pass.

This system doesn't seem valid to me at all, because it is a false comparison. You can't take a child with this kind of background, educate him according to his ability all year long, and then expect him to come up to grade level on a national standardized test. It's ridiculous. We did a lot of messing around and a lot of retesting and finally we used a test more suited to these children which would have made sense in the first place.

I can't see any use in having many of my children repeat the sixth grade. They would hate it so much that they probably wouldn't learn much next year anyway. They would certainly be problems and they might not get any better teacher than they had this year. I think that all of them will probably go on except Richard who is a very disturbed child.

I get very upset when I find that some people don't seem to understand the problems of our people here. They seem to feel that Welfare is a give-away program and that the lower class deserves to be lower class because they don't work hard enough. They don't understand that some people are born into circumstances so hard and so difficult that they can't climb out of them. I used to feel that way too. I felt that if you worked hard and did a good job, no matter who you were or how little you started with, you could better yourself and become prosperous and even wealthy. In my contact with these people, and in all I've learned about poverty and economic conditions in this country, I realize that there is really very little that an individual can do unless he is able to get a good education. And he's got to have a lot of help to do that.

Not long ago I read a letter in the *Monitor* that stated that lower-class families are getting more for their tax dollars than upper-class families. This and other things in the letter seemed so ignorant that I wrote an answer to it. I just wanted to make it clear that it is our job and duty as citizens to see that these families get the same breaks that other families in our city have. I don't know whether or not it did any good, but this is what I wrote:

In a recent letter entitled "The Paying Class" Mrs. S_____ says that: "lower-class families are getting more for their tax dollars than the upper-class families." It does not seem so to me. I am a schoolteacher in a large city. Most of my Negro and Puerto Rican children do not enjoy more than most middle-class children. In fact, they are deprived of many rich experiences that should be theirs as citizens of a rich and beautiful country.

They come to school poorly clothed and often without breakfast. If there were no free lunch or free milk they might be very hungry. Their parents are not able to share books, talk, or time with them. It is very hard to support poor families of seven, eight, or nine. More than half of my children are on Welfare. Poverty and ignorance do not breed intelligent thinking or intelligent raising of families. Yet, even in the midst of very, very little, I have found parents who sincerely want more for their children. They know that the "more" is better education.

No one knows better than they how vital it is to be able to read and write and graduate from school. Jobs depend on reading and writing and graduation diplomas.

Mrs. S_____ says, "Better education comes from desire and work." I would say desire and work come from better education. Children must be taught to want what is good for them. Children must be taught to work for that good. Desire for education does not exist in us at birth. We are taught to value it. But when a child's parent discusses little with his child, does not read himself, has no books or magazines in the home, the child does not readily understand the worth of learning to read. When there is little real conversation in the home, no intelligent discussing of issues, only the noise of the television and many quarrels, a child learns inattention.

The schools then are faced with the jobs that are usually the home's. Schools must not only teach the disciplines but the love of learning that motivates and stimulates to greater accomplishment. They must also teach the child to listen. The school's job becomes tremendous. Therefore, the school must have the support of able citizens.

The school in which I teach is fifty years old. It was originally a junior high school; it is now a renovated elementary school. We have too few books and they are frequently the wrong books. No music or art or gym teacher comes to the room as in suburban classrooms.

To foster a love of learning and school in children, our schools, especially in the depressed areas, must benefit by all the research and money and experts our nation has. These schools are being more than schools. Sometimes they are homes. It is imperative we equip them for the work thrust upon them.

The next question I hear people asking is, "But why should I, who work hard, have to pay for the children of people who don't work hard." I say, "Why do strong people always have to help weak people, healthy people, sick people, and rich people, poor people." We who have learned the value of work and right desire must teach that value to those who haven't learned it yet. We must teach. What better place than in the schools to fight ignorant thinking and weak effort? It is in the schools that we fight to make all Americans self-disciplined and self-supporting.

3

"But you care about them..."

"Sometimes I feel it's
almost impossible to be
as creative in your ap-
proach to teaching these
children as they require.
But you care about them,
so you keep on working,
trying to give them the confidence they need and
cut down on their frus-
tration and hope you can
help them succeed."

My experience working at the Bureau of Child Welfare influenced me to want to become a teacher. I found I enjoyed working with people, especially children. I like teaching in a deprived area. I feel I now understand very well the home environment of these children and the problems they face. School experience is extremely important to these children. With proper encouragement and guidance I feel they can be helped to develop their potentials and I want to help provide this guidance.

I got into social work mostly by accident; I graduated from college with a major in anthropology and little possibility of employment in that field. There were occasional openings in museums, but they were few and far between. One of my friends told me that it was possible to get a job in the Welfare Department without any experience so I tried that. Luckily, I was assigned to the Bureau of Child Welfare instead of the Bureau of Public Assistance. I found I enjoyed it.

In the Bureau of Child Welfare, we were concerned with making arrangements for the care of children whose mothers were incapacitated either temporarily or for long periods. If a mother was going to the hospital for a week or two, planning wasn't too difficult. We could arrange short-term shelter care or for a homemaker to come into the home and take care of the children, and that would be the end of the case.

But in instances where a mother was chronically incapacitated because of severe physical or mental illness or because of family instability, we had to make other plans for the children such as foster care, occasionally adoption, or we worked out plans with relatives.

We also worked with children who were retarded or disturbed and arranged for psychiatric treatment. This was a long, drawn-out process, because our facilities were so limited. Children would have to wait a year or longer before being admitted to a residential treatment center. Meanwhile, the situation at home deteriorated further, the school situation would be difficult, and yet we couldn't do anything but wait.

Casework presented tremendous problems to me. Theoretically, agency rules had to be followed. I had a lot of personal difficulty with this because I always wanted to make exceptions for the families with whom I was working. We had close supervision and were not allowed to make exceptions; I didn't like this. You have to be objective, of course, because that is really the only way you can help, but it was a continuous struggle not to become more emotionally involved with my clients.

You couldn't lose your concern for these people, it was with you all the time. I began to feel depressed and disillusioned, because I realized that the help we could give was only temporary and so limited. We could perhaps help the client get over a difficult period, but we could not change the basic circumstances that brought about the problem—poverty, ignorance, illness—in a vicious cycle. We knew the client would be back again with the same problem, or another one, because the basic underlying problem was not solved by the help provided by the agency. Most of the clients were trapped in their circumstances and many of their children seemed headed in the same direction. I would get to know the children and I couldn't bear this to happen. The longer I worked, the more I became convinced that these problems would be solved more by education than by social work.

By the time we got to work with the people, it was usually too late to give any kind of permanent help. There was little I could do. These people were often living in decaying tenements with an allotment of maybe $7.00 a week per person plus rent from the city, and of course their children were going to have problems. I kept worrying about the children —I didn't want them to be thrown into the same pattern as their parents.

My parents worried about my job, but I never had any trouble when I visited my clients in their homes. In some ways I think the teacher has to deal with children as the social worker does with her clients; if you ask for trouble— that is, if you are hostile and demanding—you can get into difficulty. But if you really listen and show understanding and do not unduly force your authority, you won't have any problems.

As a social worker, I had to visit the school of any child who needed foster care. We had to visit the teacher to find out how the child was adjusting scholastically and socially. I looked forward to going into the classroom on these visits.

Because of our tight schedule, I would often make a school visit without an appointment if I were in the neighborhood. The teacher would have to leave her class. Sometimes I didn't get more than five minutes but, since the teacher saw the child every day, her comments were generally perceptive.

If the child involved was disturbed, as well, I would speak with the guidance counselor, too. The schools wanted to discharge the child who was a problem. They would put a lot of pressure on me, because they couldn't cope with the child in school. The guidance counselors were terribly overworked. There was not much they could do, anyway, because, by the time a child was referred to us, he was beyond the type of help he could get from a guidance counselor. Therefore we were almost always under pressure to remove the child. It was very discouraging.

At the end of my third year at the Bureau of Child Welfare, I had my vacation the last two weeks of August. As soon as I left my job, I knew I didn't want to go back. I wasn't exactly sure what I wanted to do, but after my vacation I gave notice. I thought about going back to school because I didn't have any special kind of training. I was going to register for my master's in archaeology, then I considered social work school.

Then one day, the idea of teaching suddenly seemed greatly appealing. I had found through my job that I enjoyed working with children. I felt that a teacher, who had such continuous close contact with children, could do more for them than the social worker. And I also felt pretty certain that if I obtained my master's degree in the city I would be assigned to a city school. I had many friends and relatives teaching in suburban schools, but I knew I didn't want to teach there. I had heard that the big concerns there were producing projects and productions to impress the parents. I wanted to learn to teach children.

I guess I was the last one admitted to the preservice program that year. My admission was facilitated because I had already been admitted to the university's graduate school following my graduation from college. I had been taking some courses in anthropology while I worked.

During my first semester in the preservice program, I was in a school where there were mostly underprivileged children. I didn't do much teaching. Maybe I did less than most other students, I don't know. It was all very new. Just going back and sitting in a classroom was enough change for quite a while. It was a big adjustment in the beginning. The educational lingo was so very new that, initially, I had trouble understanding the readings and lectures. By November, I think, I was acclimated—at least, to theoretical education. But as for actual teaching, I know I couldn't have done much of it that first semester. I was still very unsure and hesitant.

I did teach a lesson on Mexican history in a sixth-grade class. I talked about the Aztecs. I remember all the preparation I did. That got me excited about teaching. I realized I would have to learn so many things very thoroughly. Not just generalizations because that wouldn't be enough. You had to dig into things and be very exact and clear so the children would understand. Gradually I began to get a little feeling of confidence about being up in front of the class. I enjoyed that. And I began to feel that I was more interested in really teaching the various kinds of subject matter, too.

I was a little disappointed in the atmosphere of the school where I did my second semester of student teaching. The teachers were very "clique-ish," and it was difficult to get to know them. You could go for weeks and see only a few of the teachers. I had a wonderful cooperating teacher, however. She was friendly and easy to get along with. She made my student teaching assignment very pleasant. I think a lot of the things I do now are things I learned from her.

It was a good thing that she never left me alone with her class, because it would have been chaos. I don't think the children would have listened to me. They were pretty much attached to her. They accepted me because I was someone new who had time to give them individual attention, and because she encouraged them to, but they adored her and that was as it should have been.

When I was ready to graduate, I was still very apprehensive about my ability to organize a classroom. I felt that I still needed to know more about planning a program, particularly in reading and social studies. I didn't know how to develop and carry through a unit of work. I wasn't sure how to plan for teaching so many individuals and groups. I was encouraged by my ability to establish individual relationships with children easily. Working with a group, however, is a different matter, and I was not sure whether I could work with the entire class without sacrificing the individual attention I wanted to provide. As it has turned out, these were, in fact, the things that have given me the most trouble this year.

I didn't want to go back to the school where I did my student teaching. That place was very difficult to get to, and I wanted to work near a subway stop. I had had to travel nearly three hours every day to get to and from school, and it was tiring. I thought an extra twenty minutes would help a lot. Then, too, I always like to go someplace new.

When I began looking, I thought all the principals would be ready to grab me, but I found just the opposite. There certainly didn't seem to be the great number of vacancies I had expected. I started looking for a job about the beginning of June, I think. I thought that would be a good time because most of the principals would know by then which teachers weren't coming back in September.

I went first to three schools that were in the neighborhood that I wanted. I remembered the principals from the meeting we had when we reported on our Teaching Corps program. I thought they would be interested that I had done my student teaching in the area and wanted to teach there. But most of them never even gave me a chance to tell them anything about myself. They said, "We don't have any vacancies. If we do we'll let you know."

I went to a lot of schools. Some of the principals said that they would call me in August if a vacancy occurred then. When I was getting pretty desperate, I saw an ad in the paper for teachers. Someone told me that if a principal had to advertise there must be something wrong with the school, but I went down anyway. The principal was very cordial and gave me a tour of the school. He didn't ask me anything about teaching methods, just if I was interested in teaching these children. He asked me if I knew what the problems were, and I said I thought I did.

He told me about the school. It is a very old school in a changing neighborhood. A big middle-income housing development is being erected. There is going to be a new school building soon. The site has already been selected. But right now all the children live in the surrounding low-income projects. This has given a certain stability to the school population.

The principal gave me the impression that he loved the children and that he was very interested in them. As we walked down the hall he spoke to the youngsters, calling them by their names. He said he wanted someone who could control the classroom situation, and I got real brave and said I thought I could do that.

Even the secretaries, the first people I met, gave indication of a pleasant atmosphere. I could tell the tone of the school, too, by the way the teachers walked into the office and came right up and said "Hello." They were very friendly. Some schools I had been to had such cold, tense, atmospheres.

The principal really didn't ask me too much about myself. He told me about the school and then he said, "Do you think you would be happy teaching here?"

I thought I would, and I am—most of the time anyway.

Last summer I went to summer school and then my husband and I went on vacation for about three weeks. The two weeks before school began I spent planning what I was going to teach the first day. I came home that first night and I wasn't going back. I absolutely wasn't. I didn't know what I was going to teach the second day. I had already done everything that I had planned and I didn't know what I was going to do next.

There was quite a scene. My husband said I didn't have to go back. He said that I could stay home the rest of my life, if I wanted to. I didn't *have* to teach, even though I had spent a whole year and two thousand dollars getting ready to do it. I could quit after one day if I wanted to. He made me mad. I went back.

I had no books, no supplies. I couldn't even occupy the children with drawing as I had no drawing paper, no crayons, no reading material. I had a blackboard and chalk, and the children had notebooks, and that was about it. The teachers were very nice, they gave me what they had, if there was something extra. But they all had their books from the previous year. When they set up the new classes the previous June, the teachers put the books they would need in their classrooms, and the new supplies hadn't come in yet.

Finally I got some reading books, but there weren't enough to go around. I wasn't sure how to begin a reading program anyway. I had a friend who was teaching fourth grade in another school and whatever she did, I did—reading a poem, math drill, spelling, making a calendar, everything. There was no kind of continuity. One thing one day and another the next.

It wasn't until much later that lessons began to achieve continuity. When one step began to logically follow the next in a teaching sequence, planning became much easier and, of course, much better.

After a while I attempted to set up my reading groups on the basis of the tests given in third grade plus some informal reading tests that I had given. Mine is a 4-3 group which is a little below average for this school. When I tried to give the books out for the two groups, some of the children wouldn't accept the books I felt they were ready for. Some didn't want the pink book because they had used it in the year before and others didn't want the blue book because they could read on the book's cover that it was a second-grade book and they were now in the fourth grade. They just wouldn't take the books when I gave them to them, and a few children even cried.

So I ended up not really grouping the children. I gave the slower readers two books. A lot of them still have two readers. I now let them work with the upper group and I tell them to take the easier book home and read it. I work with the slower ones when the others are doing written work. We go over what the child has read at home and do extra drill work. When a child is so far behind, he feels better about doing it that way.

I know many teachers criticize the basal readers, but I found that my children enjoyed the stories and looked forward to reading them. Some of the stories, like those about animals, were informative, and the children really found the nonsense stories humorous. They also enjoyed reading about children who lived long ago and children living in other parts of America. We always compared and contrasted the way of life of the story children with the city life known to my children. Some children had never seen a private house; they were fascinated by backyards, playing in attics, and riding bikes along the street.

But we also discussed that children able to do these things might never have a chance to ride in an elevator or watch the boats in the harbor from their bedroom windows. Even the slower readers who couldn't understand all the words were able to follow the stories through our discussions and the pictures. They entered the discussions, too, and chuckled appropriately when reading. I think the children learned much about people and about life from these stories and their vocabularies were enriched. However, I felt other materials were needed to help the children improve their comprehension. Also, certain skills can be taught more effectively if the teaching is more individualized.

I asked for some SRA materials for next year, but I was told they had never been used in this school, and, if they were, they would be tried out first in the top class on the grade level. Then maybe that teacher could teach others how to use them. Actually, I think I know how to use them now, and

I'd like to try it. I think these materials would further motivate many of the children and help improve their skills.

We went on two trips in the first two months of school. Other teachers had set up the trips and got the buses and I was able to go along. One of these was to the zoo and the other was a ferry ride. After each of these trips, I had the children write up their own stories. It was hard because they couldn't spell the simplest words, and it took about two hours to get four sentences.

I went through each story individually with the child and made the corrections. I then typed all the stories on good white paper with a primer typewriter. I gave the stories back to the children, had each one read his own and illustrate it on another piece of paper. I put them together with cardboard covers and made our own books.

I started having some time every day devoted just to free reading. I let the children read the two trip books, and another book that we had written up about birds, following a film we had seen. I also let them read comic books and browse through magazines which I brought in and some science books with lots of diagrams and illustrations that I had borrowed from the library. I'm not sure how much reading they did but they surely wore out those homemade books. In spite of all of my Scotch-taping, they are now literally in shreds.

At the very beginning I assigned a great deal of homework, but it was homework of a sort that had a high interest level and a fairly low skill level, such as dictionary work, alphabetizing, copying things out of books. This may not seem like it would have a high interest level but actually, these children, especially the ones of low ability, enjoy doing what they call "schoolwork" and being very, very busy with pencils and pens and paper.

I made sure that every single bit of work they handed in was read, and I always tried to put a positive comment someplace on each paper. Very rarely did I ever ask a child to redo it. I was more interested in the very beginning stages of my class in trying to get each child to hand in the work and to recognize the value of handing in work, of doing work in the class, and of making it enjoyable.

Of course, not all of my class could do basic things like alphabetizing or using dictionaries. I think that is something which isn't impressed on us enough in our courses at the college. They don't teach us that these basic things have to be taught. You know that you have to teach them to add and subtract, but you don't always think about having to teach them how to look up words, arrange a paper, and write a heading. I found all of a sudden that a lot of my children couldn't use a dictionary, and I had to go about teaching that before I could expect much in the way of independent reading activities.

I feel I have to work on reading and math every day. If I spend an hour on science and don't do math—well, they have to know how to multiply. Math is such a difficult process to learn that, if I let a day go by without it, I have just lost that time. Reading and math have to have priority.

I feel my greatest satisfactions occur whenever I see a spark in the children's eyes that tells me they are grasping the ideas I'm trying to put across. I can always tell when they really get what I'm teaching because they get so excited about it. They fairly jump out of their seats to answer questions and to ask their own. It doesn't matter what subject area it is—that's the greatest satisfaction I get in teaching and it doesn't come all the time. Well, it usually comes sometime every day but it's certainly not continual. Sometimes, only one child really understands; sometimes it will be most of them, but whenever I feel that they are learning I am happy.

I try, of course, to reach all the children, but if it happens that only one child is really catching on, I will go deeper and deeper into the subject with that child before I go back and try another approach with the other children. I will take that one child just as far as he can go right then and there. Some of his excitement in learning will sometimes reach the others and spur them on, too.

I find it very difficult to teach time and space concepts. I have tried to get the children to understand how our city has grown and changed. It is changing now, and the children observe and report on the changes in the neighborhood. But they find it very hard to imagine what they cannot actually see. I say, "Close your eyes and try to imagine that all the buildings, bridges, and cars disappear and in their place is a huge forest." I show them pictures of forests and try to get them to realize that at one time, an Indian village existed where now their tall apartment houses stand, and that long ago an Indian boy may have hunted in what is now our school yard. I say, "Suppose you were an Indian boy, what would you see?" We talked about New Amsterdam and how its capture meant that the Dutch flag went down and the English flag went up. That's a pretty concrete image, I felt— but it's hard for the children to understand because the concept of different European countries is so vague. I try to do a lot of map work because I feel it's important for the children to know where they live in relation to the rest of the world. However, the names of places are very confusing to the children and I'm disappointed that I really haven't been successful even in helping most of them understand the difference between their neighborhood, their city, and their country.

We are writing many more stories now—stories about things that happened and things that didn't. We write fairy stories, science fiction, and especially stories about monsters. A lot is taken from their experiences at home. They all watch Gorgo. They love those TV horror stories. They like to retell Gorgo's adventures and make up new ones for him.

We wrote some stories about the building going on in the neighborhood and about tearing down buildings. We are studying our city and we wrote about the person who operates the crane with its big iron boom that demolishes the buildings. I said, "How does the operator feel when he is knocking things down? Would you like to be able to do that?" Then I turned it around. "You are the building. How would you feel if this thing came crashing into you? You are being torn apart and destroyed."

Writing also helps me to understand what is going on in the minds of the children and how they feel about things. Their stories are so direct and revealing. Tony writes:

My name is Tony. I am ten years old. I live in a big house. I wish I had a dog. But I do not.

My best days are composition days. I can hardly wait for the train ride home when I can read and enjoy the children's compositions. I always praise their work highly— stories of all the children are displayed in the classroom and in the corridors. Tony has found writing an outlet for expressing himself. He has always been difficult for me to handle, refusing to do what everyone else is doing. He sometimes spends an entire afternoon writing stories, mostly imaginary autobiographies:

In 1900 Tony Williams was an old, old bum. He was eating a cat that had died. A car in the street had run over the old cat and the cat had died. The cat was a very, very old cat. But when the cat was living he was the best cat Tony Williams had ever seen. He used to eat rats. Tony Williams said that when he would die he would eat him. And he did.

In 1805 Tony Williams was the President of the United States of America. He was born on Feb. 22, 1782 and he died on Dec. 14, 1832. When he was living he was a very, very big man. He was the biggest man I ever saw.

When Gorgo's mother came to fight the city, Tony Williams, President of the United States of America, told Gorgo's mother that she better get out of town very fast before he gets very angry. Gorgo's mother picked up her feet and went like the wind. And he never saw Gorgo's mother again.

This was the story of the first President of the United States of America.

We also have to help the children see and hear and feel their environment and find words to express this. The day of the blizzard the children all gathered by the window and we talked about the blizzard. Then they wrote down their impressions:

The snow looks like a marshmallow because it is soft and white.

When you take snow in your hands you feel it is soft and cold.

When the snow falls you don't hear it.

When I was coming to school I fell down because it was so windy. The wind pushed me down. And I couldn't even see because it was so windy and snowy. I like to play in the snow. When I took some snow I threw it down and then it went into my galoshes. Did this ever happen to you?

The children listened to the sounds of the city and then wrote down what they heard:

In my house I hear the people on the 15th floor screaming and playing. I want to go to their house and play with them.

I hear birds flying in the sky. And the sound to me is flp flp.

On the street cars make noise and people cannot sleep.

The machines work so loud we can't hear ourself talk. That's why we talk loud.

I can hear a building going up. It hurts my ears when it goes up.

And one child concluded, "I hear so much sounds in the city. But there are more sounds you could hear in the city if you only listen."

We studied about the moon in science. The children observed the moon each night and noted its different phases. One day they volunteered: "We saw the full moon. It was as bright as—

a potful of gold
new money
the sun shining through a window
the blade of a knife
new shoes
the Empire State Building in the sun
a diamond ring
the point of a sword
the eyes of a black cat.

This kind of image building really excites the children. They love it, and once they get going they don't want to stop.

The problem in writing and speaking is that often the children want to share experiences but are handicapped by their very limited vocabularies. Anna rode one weekend into the country. She tried to describe what she had seen. She said, "I saw some of those animals that give milk," and asked what they were called. Juan, telling about a picnic adventure asked for "the name of the bag that you take to the park."

One of the purposes for writing is to get them to use interesting words. My cooperating teacher was very good at this. She would say, "How do you feel when you are frightened?" So they would make up a situation and they would tell how it would make them feel. She would write down all their suggestions—scared, frightened, trembling, stiff, frozen—and then she would ask, "What would you do then?" They would say things like, "I would jump out the window." "I would scream."

One of the big problems is that they don't know how to spell the words they want. That holds them back. I have one little girl who leaves every other word blank. I am supposed to guess what she means and fill it in. So I put a big, big list on the board of all the words they might need. They have lots of ideas. They have more ideas than they have skills to put them on paper.

We also spend a lot of time working on handwriting. This past week I put a silly poem on the board and I wrote it in different ways. I wrote one line all squashed together and another line very big and loopy. I am very good at imitating the children's writing. I said to the children, "Read the poem." They came to a word that was written badly and hesitated. I said, "What's the matter?" Then they told me that they couldn't understand the letters.

After we had worked on reading it for about ten minutes, one boy raised his hand and said, "I know what she's trying to do. She's showing us how we write." They all looked real silly then, but they liked it. Then we went through and rewrote the poem so it would be easy to read. I did this a few times, but you have to have a crazy poem of some kind—

tongue-twisters or nonsense rhymes—so that they want to read it and yet they find out why they have difficulty. Then I talk about the importance of concentrating on things like spacing, size, slant, and correct formation of letters.

My children are very interested in writing the correct way. At the beginning of the year they wanted me to put "Good" or "Very good" on everything they wrote. Now they don't want written comments. They never want me to put red marks on their papers. So they read their stories to me and I go over the material with them because they can't proofread their own work yet. Sometimes they work together and proofread for each other. They help each other and they love it.

I read a lot of poetry. Actually I often use the suggestions that are in the basal reader after every story. Of course now they want to make some poems of their own, too.

First, it was just rhyming. To them that is what poetry is. You read them some poems and you see how they love things like A. A. Milne because of the words. I took four words—know, glow, run, fun—and I told them that they could make any arrangements they wanted. They made their own four-line poems and they drew pictures to go along with them.

Then I gave them two words and let them build around them. I got things like:

> I can see a rabbit hop
> He can hop
> On the top of my can.
> I have a brother named Dan.

You know they are fitting words and it has nothing to do with the price of anything. Very simple but they are at least beginning.

> I saw a boy who had a box of snow
> The boy said, "I can blow the snow."
>
> A boy told me to run
> To have a lot of fun.

When they couldn't fit their rhyming words in at the end of a line they got terribly frustrated. So I said, "All

right, if you have more that you want to say, continue it."
They came up with some pretty sharp stuff.

Here is one that we worked on together so it comes out even with a meter and a rhythm to it. It has very, very simple rhyming. It is called "Spring Is Here"

> Winter is past and spring is here
> The sun is hot and the sky is clear
> The birds come back from their homes down
>   South
> The mamma must fill her baby's mouth.
> The children stayed out to play a game.
> What do they care if it started to rain?

We started off with rhymes because they are familiar and the children think this is poetry. Then we went into other things like poetry that used a lot of colorful and descriptive words. "Look through your window. Look at the bridge and the river. Think of all the words that would describe this. Now let us put it in a poem." You can also have poems that tell short, little stories.

Here's one that is out of one little girl's own mind. It's really a rather unusual little thing because it's got a story and a moral, and it's also got a form of rhythm.

> My smile is a frown
> Because my smile is upside down
> I wear it every day.
> I really don't know why
> It must be the moisture in the air
> That makes me this way.
> Even though I try to make an effort
> To be a good girl each day
> To help my friends and neighbors
> In each and every way.

There are so many exciting things like poetry that can be done with the children, but it takes experience and confidence. The hardest part is that you have to think on your feet to take advantage of the unexpected questions and ideas the children bring up. You also have to have confidence that you can get them involved in the activity and that it will be worthwhile to them.

I have worked on the writing of stories and poems by myself, but I was glad to have help with my gym classes. I handled them by myself the first half of the year, but the gym teacher helped me to get organized. We did the same thing every week. Each group had its particular place to go and knew what it was going to do. The boys threw basketballs and the girls jumped rope. I had thought we might have races and team games, but it didn't work because I couldn't set up a new routine each week. This way, when we did the same thing every week, the children knew what they were going to do and they were happy. They have improved a lot in basketball, too. The first time they tried none of them could make a basket but now they can make them quite often, and they're so proud.

As a kid I used to hate gym. But these children love it. They really look forward to it, even the most studious ones.

This term the gym teacher is doing dancing with them and the boys don't like to admit that they want to go. They don't want to touch a girl. Tony pulls his arms up into his shirt sleeves so his partner has to hold onto the cuffs of his shirt. They keep saying, "Why can't we have gym with you all the time. Why can't we play basketball?" But it's a big help to me to have him take them.

Our new assistant principal has helped me, too. He looks over our plans each week and he noticed that I wasn't doing much with health and safety. I had done the obvious things, eyes and nutrition and things like that. Then I just left that section of my plan blank. I told him that I couldn't think of anything else to do.

He said, "We'll do two things. First, I'll see if I have any textbooks and, second, I'll make a list of some suggested topics." He came up Friday with a health book and said I could have a set for the class and he'd give me the list on Monday. Of course, I can't use the book with the class. It is called "Between Eight and Nine" and the first story is about an eighth-birthday party. My kids are between nine and eleven and they'd be insulted. But I can use it myself and change it. It will be a real help.

The assistant principal has helped me, too, in coping

with children who are behavior problems. One child I couldn't cope with at the beginning of the year was James. This child would defy me continually. If I asked him to remove his sweater, he would keep it on. Of course, the other children noticed, and they waited for me to make James obey. But I couldn't. James simply remained adamant. Nor could I persuade the child to talk when I took him aside to try to speak with him. The same kind of behavior carried over into work areas. I couldn't get James to do anything. The other children began to catch on, and I knew they thought I was weak because James was so obviously the boss. Well, once I told James he couldn't have his turn at painting some shelves until he finished his work. At this he became so enraged he threw a tantrum. Later, our guidance counselor recommended that James be transferred to another class. Our guidance counselor is very fine. She is quick to recognize and help the teachers deal with problem children.

James' new teacher has no trouble with him. He is very obedient there. Of course I feel that I failed with James, but at the same time I am very relieved that I no longer have to cope with him. The funny part about this whole situation is that, on Valentine's Day, James came to my room with his big, liquid brown eyes shining and presented me with a hand-made Valentine. I can't understand it— when he was in my class, James just tortured me. But that was my fault. I didn't know how to handle him.

The problem I now have with Ramon is similar. Ramon will start bothering and swearing at other children, and I don't know how to put an immediate stop to it. Pretty soon he gets out of hand. I referred him to guidance and the counselor spoke with his mother. She feels that very little can be done because the mother doesn't recognize any problem. It is a very strict home—the child is beaten whenever he doesn't obey immediately. He is the oldest, and he has three younger brothers. After the children come home from school they are told exactly what to do until they go to bed. They do their homework together and have supper. They watch television for an hour, then all take baths and go to bed.

The child doesn't have a chance to do a thing that he wants to do or to use his own mind. Then he comes to school and I say, "Everyone take out your notebook and start this math work." Sometimes he'll do it but sometimes he won't —something he wouldn't dare to try at home. If I leave Ramon alone he starts trying to get my attention. He pokes himself with his pencil, flexes his arms, and hits himself in the head. He says he can't work because he doesn't know how to do the work. He complains aloud that "the teacher gives us too much to do." Soon he begins to mouth curses at the other children. When I tell him to get busy and do his work Ramon says, just loud enough for all to hear, "I'm making the teacher angry. She's getting angry. I'm making her angry." Of course, I *am* getting angry, but I can't stop him. He's a big child and physically I don't frighten him. If I scold, he retaliates by mumbling and swearing. The other children will say, "Oh, Ramon said a bad word." I understand why Ramon behaves as he does, but I don't know how to cope with him in class.

Ramon told me one day that he wished he had a man teacher who would beat him if he didn't do his work. I said, "Would you want me to do that?" He said, "Yes, I would."

The assistant principal has really been very helpful with Ramon. He takes him down to the office and talks with him. I feel that I have some backing, and I am more comfortable about it. I heard about one assistant principal who told his teachers not to send kids down to him. He said, "If you can't handle your own class then you might as well teach somewhere else or forget about teaching." Our assistant principal seems to feel that it is his job to help us when we need it. He is willing to take on that resposibility. I have tried to learn to control my own class, but there are times when I am really grateful for assistance.

I have children whom I never touch. I have children whom I never scold. Tony is one. When I have a problem with him, it is only aggravated if I scold or get angry. He is the kind of child who will come up and tap me on the shoulder when I am teaching the class and say "Look at this," and expect me to give him my complete attention at that very moment. If I don't, he becomes angry and makes a lot of noise.

I know Tony needs recognition and constant approval, but how can I give this to him without neglecting the others? Private talks while others are working, some time during lunch hour, and a chance to have all the children listen to him while he relates a long-winded but interesting tale help a little, but Tony seems to want my attention most when I can't give it to him.

Every child needs special handling. Little Paul, physically smaller and much less robust than the others, compensates by trying to act "big" in class. He shouts out answers right or wrong. When I reminded him the other day that we don't call out, he laughed through his *Weekly Reader,* which he had rolled up into a tube. Another time, when told if he called out the answers he would be ignored, Paul retorted, "Then I'll shout them out."

Many of these children, like Paul, behave the same way at home. Their parents can't cope with them either.

Although I do have problems handling some of the children, most of the youngsters are respectful and want very much to be cooperative and helpful. Pamela writes, "Happiness is being good to our teacher." Roberto apologizes in a note: "I know I should listen to you Mrs. _____. I won't fool around in class again." Nancy writes for a spelling sentence, "It is hard to manage a bad boy."

Many children will respond to just a very quiet voice, but it takes endless patience. Sometimes when I'm ready to yell at them, I say, "Do you want me to raise my voice? Do you want me to yell at you?" They have heard me shout and they know it isn't very pleasant, so they are very pleased to get a warning. That's sometimes just as good as yelling.

Anyway, when my voice gets loud, they shout right back. My voice gets louder, and theirs get louder. But if I begin to talk low, they talk lower, too. Sometimes you can almost make them whisper that way. I am sure that something is accomplished because you are not getting any better results when you shout.

I did start out being very firm but by the end of the first

week I let down. Of course, everybody said "Don't," but the children were so well-behaved that first week. I thought it would continue. But it didn't. As soon as one child dared disobey and nothing drastic happened to him, others quickly caught on. Sometimes a very firm teacher is exactly what they would like. Some of the teachers don't allow any talking or moving around during work periods.

But certain children, I feel, have special needs, and I want them to have the individual attention and handling they crave. Sometimes I say no one is to get out of his seat and then there will be one child who has to throw a piece of paper away. I know that the desks are really too small and it's not an unreasonable thing to do. But as soon as one child is allowed to get up, it's amazing how many things suddenly need to be thrown away.

I used to feel that the children should know how to behave, and that, if I said to them—"You know that isn't right," they would know. But they don't. After I realized that, we talked about good manners, made up a good-manners checklist, and talked about why we needed to have good manners. I was amazed at how quickly such disturbing habits as slamming doors and loudly crumpling paper disappeared once we discussed it and tried some role playing. We would have a child stomp noisily around the room and then slam the door on his way out while the others listened. Then another child would get up and leave quietly, and we would discuss how the two kinds of behavior made us feel. The children caught on quickly and after this they took to reminding each other not to slam the door and those nearest the door would jump up to hold the door back if a child forgot.

It wasn't so easy, though, to correct calling out. I used written situations with questions like these:

> Jane really wanted to learn to do math. But every time the teacher called on her to answer a question Bill would shout out the answer. Jane never had a chance to think out the answer herself. She never even had a chance to find out if she knew the right answer.
> How do you think Jane felt?

What would you say to Bill if you were Jane? What do you think Jane's teacher should do?

Tom's father had given him a new book for his birthday. It was about animals and had big pictures in color of tigers, lions and leopards. Tom brought it to school because he wanted to show the pictures to the children in his class and share the book with them. The teacher asked Tom to come to the front of the room to show the book. But as Tom started to show the book to the children Juan and Danny began to whisper and fool around. Tom talked louder but it was hard to explain about the book when other children were talking.

How do you think Tom felt?

What would you do if you were Tom?

What do you think Tom's teacher should do?

I gave each child a copy of the stories to read. We talked about them. Then we acted them out. Afterwards, the children answered the questions. They wrote, "Tom felt unhappy." "Jane felt mad." "I would say, 'Please Bill don't shout out the answer'." "I would tell the teacher to keep them quiet." "I would say, 'Shut up'." "I would tell Bill that he did not have manners." "I would say, 'We know you know the answer but keep quiet'." Ramon wrote, "I would have a fight." The children thought the teacher should, "scold them so they will learn a lesson," "scream at the children," "talk to the boys' mothers," "send them to another class," "put them in the first grade because the first grade calls out like babies," "make them write one hundred words ten times each." Juan wrote, "The teacher should tell the children that are talking, 'stand up, I will pop you in the face'." Ramon wrote, "Tom's teacher should hit him."

Although in talking and writing about these situations, the children readily identified improper behavior and were quick to suggest retribution, in practice there was little carry-over of this. Calling out and inattention to others continues to be a big problem.

Anyway, we made up a good-manners chart and I bought some of those flag stickers to mark the children's progress.

Actually, I figured fourth-grade children wouldn't like that kind of incentive, but they were thrilled. One child said to me, "Last year we had stars and that was nuttin'."

The first day the chart was posted, the well-behaved children behaved well, as usual, and the others called out and fooled around, as usual. I thought the idea was going to be a flop, because when I gave out the flags at the end of the day the problem children began to say, "Oh, who wants those old flags anyway. They're cheap." The well-behaved children began to hesitate about accepting them. Then I gave a flag to one of the class leaders. He accepted it eagerly, and suddenly all the children wanted flags. I knew then that the idea would work—and it has. Now everyone wants a flag and the children count how many they have every day. Some of them are making more effort to follow the class rules. They even study the world map to decide which flags they want next. I hated to use this kind of motivation for good behavior, but to the children it is very concrete and fair and they understand it.

But of course it doesn't solve all my problems. If a child misbehaves at nine-thirty in the morning and knows he isn't going to get a flag, he is going to be especially bad the rest of the day. You just have to work along with that.

I do have something in my classroom that has been a big help when children get upset and I discovered it quite by accident. There is a large pipe at the back of my room and someone had wedged a broken chair in behind it. One day after Carlos threw a tantrum, he ran back to the pipe, crawled in behind it and curled up on the seat. I knew he needed to stay there and I left him alone. Now when a child becomes disruptive I tell him to stand in the back of the room. Usually he will crawl in behind the pipe. There he can sulk in private. Often children will just voluntarily leave their seats and crawl in behind the pipe. I never stop them. When they feel better they poke their heads around the pipe and begin to participate in the classwork. Soon they voluntarily return to their own seats. That chair looks pretty awful in my room but I wouldn't move it for the world.

Next year I am going to be a little firmer. I can be. I could do it now but I would have to be so tight with them that it wouldn't be a happy situation. I came in one day and was a real tyrant. I changed the whole tenor of my class. For about two days there was no talking at all—absolutely none. The children worked all morning in silence and all afternoon. The children didn't seem to be particularly sad but they became kind of apathetic. Few children volunteered to talk which was most unusual as my class is usually very communicative —there's a lot of give and take. I was very uncomfortable —the tension in the classroom was unbearable. I couldn't keep it up.

I guess I haven't yet been quite able to make up my mind just what kind of a classroom atmosphere I would like. I am very concerned about individuals, and I can't make rules and stick to them because I'm always seeing exceptions—the way I did when I was working for the Bureau of Child Welfare. But I keep thinking that it would be nice to have a very well-organized, orderly classroom like those of some other teachers I know. I think you have to have both. You need to have enough structure to keep the routines going but you have to have a lot of flexibility, too. I don't know how to get it though. This is my big concern.

But in spite of all my failures, my children like school. They write that they like school because ". . . you learn a lot of things in school."

". . . we go on trips."

". . . it's more fun than outside."

". . . I could make a puppet."

". . . I like to learn."

Roberto, who wrote, "No, I don't like school because you have to wake up early and because we get too much work," added, "In some ways I like it."

Staying in after school isn't a punishment—it's a privilege. I've been taken aback when, in an attempt to quiet them down, I've said in what I thought was an angry, threatening voice, "And who wants to stay in this afternoon?" The chorus of "Oh, me! Please me!" always throws me. The children are always anxious to help after school or during the lunch hour—but doing regular classroom jobs is another matter. I had some real difficulty getting boys to accept such jobs as erasing the blackboards and taking the basket around. They complained, "Man, I'm no slave" and "I ain't no garbage man."

But most of the children would like to be good in school. They enjoy the satisfaction of being successful and having the approval of the teacher just like anyone else. They write, "Happiness is learning something." "Happiness is getting one hundred on a spelling test." "Happiness is getting 'Excellent' on my report card." Even Ramon wrote, "Happiness is being smart in school."

When the mothers come to see you they are concerned mostly about school behavior. They always want to know if their child is behaving. They equate being good and academic achievement. Most of the parents have no idea what kind of work their child is doing on a day-to-day basis unless the teacher sends a note home. I have tried to encourage the children to bring home their classwork and show it to their parents and talk to them about it but this is a strange idea to them. Many children don't expect their parents to look at their work or show that they care except at report card time. It's really amazing how much these children accomplish all on their own.

That's why I think the teacher's attitudes are so important. If children meet teachers who are prejudiced, who aren't interested in them, or think that they can't learn, they become discouraged and drop out of school. Everything in their environment is against their continuing in school so to a large degree it is really up to the teacher to help them overcome their environment.

Sometimes I feel it's almost impossible to be as creative in your approach to teaching these children as they require. But you care about them, so you keep on working, trying to give them the confidence they need and cut down on their frustration and hope you can help them succeed.

I think, though, that the parents are beginning to realize how important the schools are. They are becoming more interested in the school program and are beginning to try to do something about getting better schools for their children.

The Civil Rights boycott of the city schools really publicized the education issue and made the parents much more aware of what the schools are trying to do and its importance to each one of them. In our area the boycott seemed to be focused more on the idea of improving poor schools than of integration.

It's pretty hard to take all the publicized antagonism to the schools when you know that you are doing the best you can. I didn't feel very good about the teachers' stand, or lack of stand, during the boycott, however. I'm still bothered about what I did.

The morning of the boycott I got to school about ten after eight. There were about twelve pickets around the school and a lot of other parents. Three of our teachers were in the picket line. Everyone was very jovial and seemed to be enjoying it. There wasn't a child in sight.

A good many of the teachers were wavering between going into the school and not going in. It was funny to watch. The pickets were at the front door, and most of the teachers who wanted to go in went around to where they couldn't be seen, through the side door. The ones that did use the front door went in with an almost defiant attitude. They would run up the steps and go in without even looking around at the pickets. They didn't even acknowledge that the pickets were there.

One of the teachers pointed out that, really, it's too bad that the teachers went in that way. This was a chance to talk to some of the parents, to find out how they were feeling, but we didn't do it. I think the parents were perfectly understanding of our going to work. I think they would have preferred that we didn't go in but I don't think they resented that we did.

I had three children in my grade that day—one Negro, one Chinese, and one Puerto Rican. They told me they came because they wanted to come to school. All of the other children stayed away; they were afraid of what would happen. One of my toughest boys told me that he and his friends started to come to school, and then began to talk about what would happen when they got there. They were afraid that there would be fighting, so they turned around and went home.

I think the reaction of the children afterwards when we talked about it in class was interesting. I asked them what they had done all that day. Our neighborhood was completely deserted from the morning until after three o'clock when we went home. There was not a child outside the school and the playground was empty. Most of them said that they stayed in their apartments. Some of them had gone out with their parents. When I asked them why they were out of school they had no idea of what it was all about. One said that his parents kept him out because they were afraid of trouble, but most of them had nothing at all to say about it—I mean, just *nothing*. Didn't they know, or did they think it best not to tell their white teacher?

We had a faculty meeting in our school a few days before the boycott and tried to decide what to do. The point was brought out about teachers being very involved and threatening to go out on strike for better wages and better teaching facilities; yet when the boycott came it didn't seem to hit so close to home. This wasn't really happening to them.

Segregation is not primarily the school's fault, not in the beginning. I think there may have been some unwise building of schools and bad zoning but basically it is an economic problem where people are forced to live in certain areas and this causes the problems.

One of the pickets had a flyer he was giving out and on it were the basic complaints: classes were too large—they should be limited to twenty children, there were not enough textbooks, teaching was not adequate, proper teaching materials were not supplied, the schools are too old. There were about ten complaints like that. These are exactly the same things that the teachers have been working for—there was just one thing in the list of grievances about integration— they really did want all the things the teachers want.

It means reorganizing the whole school system so it functions more efficiently. The way to do it is to get rid of these poverty-stricken schools in the lower-class areas of the city. But it can't be done just like that, because it would take a tremendous expenditure of money.

I think that the real thing that was accomplished by the boycott was that people were forced to think—everyone had to think about education. Segregated schools are unequal schools because of what they do to a child's image of himself. When we're improving schools that are segregated, we can't just leave it there. I don't know what we are going to do about it but I don't think we are going to make much progress in improving education in depressed areas until we find out.

4

"I'm glad I stuck it through...

. . . I'm very proud that
I'm going back to the
same school next year.
I feel that if I take
something on, no matter
how hard it is, I've got
to see it through to the
end. I guess it all
adds up to one thing.
People expected a lot of
me and I tried to live
up to their expectations."

I can't really remember when I began to think about being a teacher. My mother was a teacher and a guidance counselor, and my grandmother and my uncle and aunt were teachers, so, at first, it was just assumed that I would teach, too. Later, I thought about journalism and social work but I always gravitated back toward teaching. Maybe I felt it offered more security, but there were other inducements. I wanted to work with people; that was the most important thing to me. I had to decide what sort of people I wanted to work with. Finally, I chose to work with children.

There was never any doubt in my mind or in my parents' minds about my going to college, but there was a lot of talk about what kind of college it would be. We decided against a teachers college because my parents felt I was too close to teaching. We chose, instead, a liberal arts college, and I'm very glad. I didn't want to have as friends only people who were going to be teachers. I wanted to meet people who were going to be political scientists, lawyers, writers, and doctors. I wanted to come in contact with people who had other interests than my own.

I really wanted to go to a big university, but I ended up in a small college mostly because I didn't want to wait to be accepted. Also, Hillford was just beginning and I was impressed by the new buildings, the small ratio of students to professors, and the pioneering spirit that everyone seemed to have.

Academically, it was really very rough. Hillford was trying to build a name and a reputation fast and the students were under great pressure. We were told that no one was interested in our social lives or in our ability to hold a teacup properly. Everything was academically oriented, everything. Even so, I have no regrets at having gone there. I had the finest academic education I could have gotten anywhere.

The school did nothing to provide for the personal needs of the students, however. We tried to make up for that by organizing a lot of things for ourselves. I had a million jobs. I was secretary of the student government for three years

and class secretary for two years. I was also a student counselor in charge of a floor of girls—freshmen, sophomores and
juniors—for one year. It was hard, because I knew all of the
girls well and, knowing me so well, they felt they could get
away with a lot of things. This presented a lot of conflicts.
Having taken on a responsibility, I felt I had to go through
with it. It was a good experience, because I had never had
any authority over people near my own age; when I was a
camp counselor, the girls in my charge were much younger.

I was the only one of my college group who went into
teaching. My mother looked up graduate programs in the
education field for me and sent me many brochures. I got my
provisional admission to graduate school on the third of
May. My father said, in a letter, "Now you're in. They've
taken your money and they can't do anything else." It wasn't
as easy as that, however, because I knew that I really had to
make good—after all, the admission *was* provisional.

I told myself how hard I was going to have to study. I
took eight points of work in the summer. The school required
a B average in fifteen credits for admission to full graduate
standing. I felt that I had to do that for myself to make up
for my rather average undergraduate record. It was a challenge that forced me to do my best.

The summer session gave me a very good introduction
to graduate school. There were two good courses which I
really liked. I came to class every day and worked hard. The
whole program really impressed me. I was coming into contact with people who had been other places. I had had a very
limited background, and all of this was very exciting. I'm
glad I started graduate work right after college. I was still
in a mood to work. Then I had the summer free before starting to teach the next year; that was good, too.

We had more than ordinary people in our seminar the
first semester. They were energetic, superb people—a very
intelligent group. We worked all semester in really close
contact. We felt that we were doing a lot more than the
people in other seminars even before our special project
started.

We had been discussing the community-study project, and
a lot of us began to talk about doing something different. I

thought it would be fun to make a film, and a lot of the others thought it would be a good idea. When we spoke to our college advisor about it, he had some reservations because of the time and the expense involved and because we didn't really know what we wanted to put in the film.

After a lot of talking and planning, Mr. Copeland got us a movie camera from the college, and we each chipped in five dollars to buy film. As time went on, some in the group lost a lot of their interest. They were more scientific-minded, while two of us were interested in writing, taking pictures, and that sort of thing. These were the things we had done at college.

Of course, we made an incredible number of goofs in the filming. The whole seminar group got up early one morning and went down to the school to take pictures. After the film was all developed, we discovered that none of it was any good. That sort of finished the picture-taking for a lot of the group.

Everyone helped when it came to splicing the film and getting the narration written up, though. It is really exciting to go into a field you don't know anything about and be responsible for turning out a product. This couldn't be hit or miss. It *had* to fit. If it didn't, we'd have nothing. That's the reason some in the group kept on with us even though they didn't have as much interest. We were responsible for getting out something that could prove useful. In the end, everyone helped.

It was a tremendous learning experience. I had never before worked with that medium. None of us had. It gave me a lot of good ideas and I am determined to make another movie of the school where I am teaching now. Whether or not I ever do it, I learned a tremendous amount from that project.

We learned a lot about the community, and we talked with many of the people on the streets, in the stores and in homes. So many things that we didn't put in the film were important to our understanding. We made tapes of our interviews with members of the Parents Association. They were so pleased that we wanted to record what they said and they were very eager to talk about their school.

The parents were very lavish in their praise of us and

in their attitudes toward us. I don't think we'd have gotten that warmth if we hadn't been working on the community study and showing them that we really wanted to know about them and their community. None of us had ever been in that section of the city before. We were really interested and we were looking for things. We saw a lot that we never would have seen if we hadn't been doing the film. For me, it was one of the highlights of the whole preservice program.

It was an unparalleled experience but at the end of the semester I told my mother that I just couldn't do this any more. It was killing me to leave my house at seven-thirty every morning, arrive home at five o'clock every evening and *then* begin homework. I was staying up very late each night and my parents agreed that I should not do it. On the other hand, it seemed to me that I would be wasting some valuable learning by not continuing. I began to feel I was putting myself above my job. At the same time, I had just about reached the end of my rope with that traveling. I guess it was just stubborness and pride that made me change my mind and join the Teaching Corps. I had gone that far. I had started something and had helped make the film that interested other people in the area. If I didn't come through —if I let the area down—then how could I expect other people to go there?

One other thing that bothered me was that I didn't know whether or not I would want to teach in the South Bay area after I graduated. How valuable would my student teaching in a city school be if I decided to teach in a suburban community? And then, how would I feel if I "deserted" the city for the seemingly easier suburbs? It was really quite a decision to make.

Of course, like the others, I was influenced largely by the pioneering aspect of the whole thing. Almost too much. I've always been like that. The thing that helped us last year was this feeling that we *were* a very special group. It made us really feel more conscientious, I think, than we would have been without it.

Had I known that I was going to get the class I got this year, I would have wanted to be assigned to a low-ability class for my student teaching. However, I didn't know, and

I think I had a very good student teaching experience; I have no complaints. As far as student teacher-cooperating teacher relationships were concerned, ours was wonderful. Mrs. Klein was more than a cooperating teacher; she was a friend. We got to be very good friends.

I really did have responsibility for the group. My cooperating teacher never showed the least bit of reluctance to give up the class to me. That happens of course, to some student teachers. I believe that one of the most admirable traits in a teacher is the ability to let another teacher take over without a feeling of resentment. It must be very difficult to be so gracious. Mrs. Klein was most constructive in her criticisms. She spent much time helping me plan lessons —more, I think, than other cooperating teachers spend with their student teachers. We'd take half our lunch periods for lunch and half the time for getting materials, or setting up experiments or writing on the board. She didn't push me out on my own, she eased me into it. She made my student teaching a most valuable experience. My parents know I just raved about her. I think that her help and the experiences I had in her room had a lot to do with my choosing that particular school when I was making up my mind about where to teach this year.

I didn't know about other schools and I wasn't that anxious to find out about them because I felt very secure where I was. I didn't go to look at any other schools at all. I wasn't lazy. I just felt very satisfied with my present situation. I knew the pitfalls of the school, but I liked the spirit of the teachers that I had lunch with. If people like that were there, the school must really have some merit. Some of them had been there five years, and they could have transferred if they really couldn't take it. They seemed to have made the adjustment. I also thought that maybe the school lacked in some things, but that perhaps I could help in some way. I don't think I have helped very much yet, but I have tried.

By the middle of May, the principal still hadn't given me any indication that he wanted me in that school. It was another big decision to make, because the school system is not the kind where you can quit and just go to another school.

Then, again, you develop emotional ties to the school, the teachers, and the children, and—regardless of an old building and poor facilities—you become part of the school. I felt that I would be cheating myself if I just left. So, when he finally asked me, I made up my mind very quickly.

It's really been a good choice. A lot of the problems are no different from those of any other school and the teachers have been so helpful. That has been a tremendous source of comfort this year. To be able to go to lunch and let everything out—to get it all off your chest and then go back in the afternoon with a different attitude and so many helpful hints—so many teachers who have gone through it have been so willing to share their ideas and materials with me. It really isn't half bad.

Last summer I went with my parents to see my sister, who lives in a nice, middle-class community. When people heard where I was going to teach, they immediately got this horrible, nightmare-like picture—pure black—and they thought I was so brave. It was really funny.

I didn't even think about teaching during those five weeks of traveling, but, when we got home, I bought the courses of study in every subject area, from arithmetic to writing, and read through every one of them. I couldn't do any planning because I didn't know yet what kind of children would be in my class. I had been told that I'd probably have the second grade. Then I got a letter saying that I would have a fifth grade. There was no information about the type of group, so I still couldn't do very much planning. I spent the remainder of the summer finding an apartment near the school so that the traveling experiences of my graduate school year would not be repeated. I was very happy and very excited.

But then school started and I had the lowest section on the grade. Do you know what that means? Over half of them are repeaters; they all know that they are in the "dumb" group, that they are "failures," and that everyone looks down on them.

I looked up their records and they were all reading at second- or third-grade level. I tried to start them in with third grade texts when I finally got some books. But they wouldn't have them. They wouldn't even try. Some of them had had the same books before and they hated them. They hated to be reminded that they were failures, and I couldn't really blame them.

The simplest—the very simplest—words were impossible for them. Everything was impossible, it seemed. If I put an assignment on the board, I had to have every word of it read aloud. There was a boy in the back of the room who copied things perfectly but when I asked him to read it back to me he couldn't read it. I had to have it read aloud and even then some of them couldn't understand it.

I needed help during those first days of school, but I didn't get it. All I got were interruptions—people coming in and handing me things and asking me to fill out things when I was trying to keep the class in order. We had three days of orientation, but in all that time we spent only twenty minutes meeting with the principal. He gave us the key to the book room and told us to take what we wanted, but I didn't know enough about my group and their needs to know what to get.

The other teachers were wonderful. They were very sympathetic, and if I asked them anything they would tell me but the trouble was that I didn't find out what I needed until I was in front of the class, and by that time it was too late. I put a sentence on the board and realized that half the class couldn't read cursive writing and the other half resisted manuscript writing because they thought it was childish. I thought I knew what to expect in a school like this—I had been here for a year as a student teacher and I had seen lots of classes. But nothing seemed to help. My class was so unruly and so impossible to discipline that I didn't sit down even for a minute for weeks. I was exhausted, and I didn't know how to help them or myself.

I remember sitting down with the curriculum bulletins, my college texts and the children's books and almost crying every night. I didn't know how to plan for a class like mine and when I went to the curriculum bulletins they were just mountains. They were such insurmountable hills to climb that I would want to just give up, because I knew I could never teach what they said I should to the group I had. It

is very hard because as a new teacher, you want to do everything the right way and it takes such a long time to know
what you can and can't do.

I think you should really know your grade curriculum,
but trying to plan the year ahead of time and trying to do
just certain things is so ridiculous. After all, you have to
start where the children are and go through to the end of
the year, not to the end of the bulletin. At least, that was
what I tried to believe.

Social studies was the hardest subject. There was a lot
of material and a thousand ways to organize it. To find the
best way for a particular class is the difficulty, and the textbook was *not* the best way for my class.

These kids needed to know something about their own
city and state and country and how these related to the rest
of the world. They needed lots of mapwork and help in physically imagining their own city in relation to the rest of the
world. They have such narrow concepts. They ride around
on their bicycles, and they know something of their own
surroundings, but they think that New York State is the
United States; when I showed them a map of the world and
tried to talk about continents and hemispheres, they got all
mixed up. Something had been left out somewhere. To get
these children to relate their city to their state and their
country was practically an impossibility, and these are very
important concepts. For a long time, I didn't do much with
social studies because they couldn't read the books, but now
I use maps and try to tell stories. I make the stories very
dramatic and then ask questions. It helps, but it is slow
work.

One of the very worst experiences is to have a child
from another class come into the room on an errand when
you are teaching social studies and say, "Oh, we did that
three weeks ago. We finished that already." And it's true.
Sometimes I walk up to another teacher and ask her where
she is in the book. If she's as slow as I am, I feel good. And
if I find someone who is fourteen chapters ahead, I feel sick
to my stomach. I'm confused and I'm afraid that next year's
teacher will think the children don't know what they should.
She will try to start with what she is supposed to be teach-

ing instead of where they are; there will be a big gap, and they won't be able to bridge it.

The class feels that it is disgrace to be behind, too. They realize that there is a schedule to be met, and other people are meeting it and they're not. They think it is terribly important. Of course, they are doing all they can, but they feel it, nevertheless. The pressure to be doing what the others do is enormous.

It shows in their feelings about taking books home. One of my youngsters remarked that, the more books you have for homework, the brighter you are. So, they want a lot of books to carry, to make it look as though they are smart. Of course, they know they aren't "smart," that they aren't in a bright class, but even carrying books they can't read helps a little. They're insulted because they don't have more homework and frustrated because they can't do what they have. So, I just let them take as many books as they wish, as long as they bring them back the next morning.

I soon learned that books weren't going to work for reading—at least not any of the books we had—so, I started to do a lot of work with phonics and developing word-building skills. I put poems, little stories, and their own experiences on the board and we read them together. We worked on phonics every day, and sometimes for most of the morning when we could use workbooks in addition to the board work. They really enjoyed the phonics and skill-building exercises I gave them.

I love that first half-hour when they all work on the things I have put on the board for them before they come in. It gives me a chance to breathe a little, to talk to a couple of the children independently, and to know that I don't have to worry about watching everyone in the room. I wouldn't change it for anything. I search for something to put on the board every morning.

In the beginning of the year, the peace and quiet didn't last very long. By eleven o'clock, no matter what I did, it was hectic. I made up my mind that I wouldn't yell. I slapped my hand on my desk to get attention, and sat and waited for them to get quiet. This worked a couple of times, but, after a while, I guess they decided that if I was going to sit there forever, they might as well make noise forever. They really aren't bad kids, but I did wonder if I was going to be able to teach them anything or if I was just going to sit there all year.

The trouble always seemed to start with little things—pushing, hitting, changing seats—and not getting anything done until finally I just couldn't stand it. I was getting impatient with academic things, too. We have been doing phonics for weeks, and when a child isn't able to figure out the word "snip" when he knows "ship," I just go out of my mind. I say, "Sit down and figure it out for yourself," and then they begin to growl back at me. I just can't help it. I have reached the limit of my patience. I really don't have much patience. I have discovered that. Maybe if I had had more patience I could have kept Eddy.

Eddy was my biggest problem, and he had to be taken out of my room. A lot of my tension is gone. I'm more relaxed, and I can go at a smoother pace. It's very odd, because there are all kinds of problems remaining in the class. Donald's still there, and so is John Herbert.

Eddy began to stand out in the beginning because I found that he was the person with the lowest reading level in the group. When I started testing for reading, I recognized that he was terribly frustrated by this. A couple of times when I spoke to him about not doing his work, he got very aggressive. He kept on getting worse, and it finally came to the point where we had no rapport. He really couldn't stand me, and I felt just about the same about him. Our personalities clashed terribly, and he made me feel aggressive, too.

Eddy destroyed everything that I was trying to do with the rest of the class; he really did. The children were very much aware that, when Eddy started something, they had all better get in their seats and do their work; they knew how upset I got over him. It was really not good for them to see me get upset like that.

I was so afraid that Eddy would start something and spoil everything for the class, that I started to pick on all the little things that he did. He felt that I wanted to get rid of him, so, naturally, he began to do big things, really big things, that no one could stand.

I guess the straw that broke the camel's back was the

incident on the way home from a trip to the neighborhood library. The children were running out into the street from between parked buses, and I was afraid that they would be hit. I said, "If you can't behave on a little trip like this in the neighborhood, I wonder how you would behave if we had to cross Fifth Avenue or go to the Museum or the 'Y'." Then I said that any person who ran into the street would jeopardize his chances of going on the next trip with us. There was another trip coming up pretty soon, and I didn't want to keep anyone home if I could help it, so I tried to warn them that way. Eddy hadn't gone on the last trip, and I knew he wanted to go on the next one very badly. I really didn't expect him to run into the street again. We had been getting along well for about a week.

Well, Eddy looked at me, and he looked at the street, and he chose the street. He ran right in front of a bus that was just pulling out. I was sure he was going to be hit—it was awfully close.

I wasn't really rough, but I grabbed him and put him against the fence that runs around the school. With that, he started to use very abusive language, and he tried to take a swing at me. He is very strong, but I held onto him and shook him hard. In the process, I ripped a button off his coat. He started shouting that I was going to pay for ripping his coat and that he would get me put out of the school. He went on and on and on.

It was awful—right in the middle of the street with people coming and going. It was just too much! The class was standing by, taking it all in, and I just felt that I couldn't go on that way any more. I'd been so afraid and had kept it all inside until I couldn't hold it any more; and now, one shove too many and I let *everything* out.

The whole class was just ruined. We never had any fun, never any jokes or good feeling. There was tension all the time. I couldn't allow any freedom at all, because I was afraid of what Eddy might do. The situation was just impossible!

I went right to see Mr. Louden and he tried to arrange to transfer Eddy to another room but it wasn't easy. No one wanted Eddy.

I guess maybe that is really Eddy's problem. He is the tenth of a family of eleven children. There is a brother in the sixth grade and a sister a year younger than Eddy. His mother is a very forlorn character. She has a heart condition, and it was very hard for her to come up to the fifth floor to visit me. She did do it once and I learned quite a bit about Eddy. She said that these were the last three of her children, and she just didn't want to be bothered anymore. She said, "I'm tired, just plain, ordinary tired. I'm getting old, and I have no husband in the home and I can't do anything about Eddy."

I spoke to the social worker and she said that she had been up to visit Eddy's family. She said that it was pretty awful. Of course, it's not for us to be snobbish and say that this is not the way to live because people *do* live that way. But you would expect people who live in a housing project to have a little bit more pride than people who live in a grubby, old tenement.

When the social worker visited, the mother just sat there with a shrug on her shoulders and talked about her oldest son who went to business school and who is her big pride. Whenever you say anything about Eddy, she will counter with, "Well, George, he . . ." I don't think that George lives in the home, but he did send me a letter about Eddy's reading and spelling. He said that it had come to his attention that Eddy couldn't read or spell, and he asked me to do something about it.

I explained to him that Eddy was getting special help in reading and that there was a homework helper program which was available for Eddy if he would go to it. I never heard from George again, but his mother certainly looks upon *him* as the one success to come out of her family. The other children had tremendous problems in elementary school. The mother used to be quite cooperative, I was told, but she finally began to feel that the school wasn't doing anything to help her, and so she stopped coming when she was called.

Eddy's school history is very, very poor, but he's not a stupid boy. He carries on a quite intelligent oral conversation and is much aware of current events and social dilemmas and racial and religious differences between people. He seems very tolerant of differences, but I wonder how he really feels. In my classroom, Eddy was a minority of one —the only child not Negro or Puerto Rican.

I don't know why he hasn't been helped by the guidance counselors. Maybe it's because his mother wouldn't cooperate. The social worker told me that she and the guidance personnel were trying to have meetings with parents of problem children but Eddy's mother never came to a session. If there isn't going to be any cooperation between the home and the school, I guess they think there's no sense working on a case like Eddy's.

Eddy had rheumatic fever when he was young, and was out of school a lot. His mother brought that up when I spoke with her. He is older than the rest of the children in the grade and more mature in a lot of ways. Because he had rheumatic fever, his mother said that physical punishment was out, and that I should give him more written homework when he didn't behave. But, of course, he couldn't do any of the written work so that wasn't going to solve anything.

If he were mentally retarded that would be one thing but he is really smart. He just has no confidence. He's been backed against a wall. I wrote all of this in the anecdotal records. I had kept anecdotal records on him since the first month of the year and they were pretty complete. I sent them down to the principal's office. At first nothing happened. Finally, I think, Mr. Louden talked to Eddy. He was better for awhile, but in the spring—after the Civil Rights boycott—he started all over again and was worse than ever. He struck me several times, and when he got into one of his tempers he was impossible to stop. So, finally, they found a man teacher who would take him and he was transferred.

Surprisingly, the class has not missed him at all. That seems very odd to me. They didn't respect him as they respect John Herbert, but they were afraid of him and they had a tendency to follow his lead. Maybe they are glad that he has gone because of the conflict between us. They haven't mentioned him at all. We have a new boy in the class—from another school—and they seem to accept the idea that he has come to take Eddy's place. I am glad they don't seem to hold any animosity toward me for Eddy's being moved.

I was afraid that might happen. It's funny that you get afraid about the things that you might hear from students. Logically, you shouldn't be threatened—emotionally or any other way—by a twelve-year-old, but no one likes to feel that he's failed.

I didn't want to give him up. I have put him down as my first year's big failure and I feel very badly that I had to give up on him. I would have liked to have kept him and worked with him but I couldn't do it.

The whole thing started off wrong. I treated him as a normal fifth grader, and I shouldn't have. I really should have gone to his mother the first time I had any problems and learned as much as I could. Then I could have adapted my class and my teaching techniques to what I learned. I'd have known that, if he wouldn't do something it would do no good to push him, because he would only get upset if I said things to him in front of the class. I should have let it slide more and talked to him in private.

I wish I had somehow found some kind of activity which would have given him some feeling of success to compensate for all the negative that was going on. I could possibly have given him more responsibility throughout the year—not as as a reward, but to let him know that I felt he was capable of it. I didn't do any of that.

As a first-year teacher, there are so many things you have to do. You're so busy trying to set up routines, decorate a bulletin board, get a sense of time, and plan activities that you really don't see your children as individuals. I have always felt that you shouldn't look at the records because you don't want to be prejudiced before meeting the children themselves, but I think I'm changing my mind. I think you should try to get all the help you can from the records, but keep an open mind when you look at them.

I needed help long before I got any, too. I think it is very important when something like this develops that the administrator of the school gets the teacher, the parent and the guidance people together to have a good heart-to-heart talk about what could be done. If I had had some help in understanding my own feelings, I wouldn't have gotten into the mess I did.

Eddy knew he had problems, but he didn't know how to

deal with them. No one was helping him. No one had helped him before he came to me, and I couldn't help him, either. He was a lost soul and I was lost, too. Now he will be going into the sixth grade still reading on a first-grade level. Nobody is stopping to help him, and he'll probably end up in trouble someday. I hope I'll never have to feel like this again.

I think it is very important to talk to parents as much as possible, but I don't seem to do it very well. I always have mixed feelings about it. It is pathetic to see how grateful a parent is to hear the least good thing about his child. Pamela's mother was almost crying when she walked out of her conference, because she was so proud that Pamela is doing well. And Pamela *is* doing very well. I was not pouring on any oil. I was telling her exactly what I meant—that I was proud to have Pamela in my class and that she was an asset to the class. I told this to Oscar's mother, too, and the look on her face was as if I had handed her a million dollars. It made me wince, because I thought maybe I did not sound sincere.

One interesting thing about the conference days was that I often saw sisters—not parents, but sisters—who were really the most responsible people I ever met. They were intelligent, inquisitive young people, and I felt as if I were talking to adults, not high school kids. It was amazing. I couldn't get over it.

But none of the mothers of my problem children ever came to see me except Eddy's mother and that was under the most tremendous pressure. Maybe that has something to do with their being problems.

I had one mother whose English was very limited, and I'm ashamed of my Spanish as she is of her English. Her daughter, who is in my class, came with her. I was very careful of my verbs and I said things slowly, and I pointed out things on papers. This mother has really been a help to me. Since we sat and talked that evening, I have had no trouble with the girl at all. The mother came a second time, too. Apparently, she values education highly.

I feel very inadequate in parent conferences because I don't know how to conduct them and my principal and all the books in the world can't help me until I have done it a lot of times. The things you have to say sound so insignificant compared with the problems they have. I read in some books at college that you should try to get background in these first conferences. But it's very hard. It sounds so funny to say, "Does he like to come to school in the morning?" "Is he enjoying school this year?" I don't know how to question a a parent delicately and tactfully in order to find out how he feels about his child, so I really don't know how to approach the situation.

I also have trouble with report-card marks. If the parent were able to analyze the report cards he would find practically nothing there. Anyhow, when I'm making out report cards, I don't know what to put down. I don't have marks for some subjects. I just have not given the children written tests. I have tested them in conversation which is not a formal yardstick of achievement. I can't test them if they can't read the questions; if they don't know what I'm asking, I can't find out anything. There are some children who never volunteer. Either they don't understand what I'm asking, or they just don't know the answer. Either way it amounts to the same thing.

The parent conferences are always tough. I get butterflies in my stomach every time I know that some parent is coming up to see me. There's one mother who has eleven children and has worked herself to death to at least let them breathe. She's so tired and withdrawn and so wrapped up in her own problems. She looks at me, standing there in my nylon stockings and my nice new dress and fresh lipstick on, and, you know, everything in place. I think to myself, "I really don't know anything," I can't get over the feeling of aloneness. I'm an outsider. Maybe it would be better if I came in a slouchy pair of shoes. It's like walking into a candy store; everyone knows right away that you can't be anything but a social worker or a teacher. You can't be a "member of the family" because of the way you dress and the way you look. I feel, then, the way I do when I put on my coat to go home and the kids rub their faces against it and talk about it's being so nice and soft. It doesn't matter that it only cost $24.95. That's not it. It's just the feeling when they look at me. I'm their ideal, and it makes me so uncomfortable. I feel that I have so much and they have so little.

On the other hand, I have to be like that and look like that in order to give them something to look up to because I represent what an educated person is. This is what the parents want for their youngsters so they want me to look different.

I have never gotten used to being looked at with admiration. I feel very uncomfortable and embarrassed when it happens. When a little girl comes in with long leather gloves because I have long leather gloves, it makes me very self-conscious.

I am very aware of how little experience I have. I can't imagine what it would be like to bring up eleven children. My parents found it hard enough to bring up two. I think about all the heartaches of trying to put a child from these families through business school or nursing school. Sometimes, when an older sister comes for a parent conference, I ask, "Are you going to school?" and she says, "Oh, yes, I am going to business school." She's so proud, and she has a right to be.

I think to myself how wonderful it is that with this impoverished background and with the tremendous needs of the family, some of them can keep so close together and be so loving to each other. There are people like Gregory with twelve children in the family—twelve of the nicest, neatest, cleanest, most polite, most aspiring children. You wonder, what do you look like to people like that? You're middle-class, urban, and very civilized, and intelligent, but you feel that you really don't know anything about life in the slums. I always feel that I may seem to be "talking down" to the parents when I want so much to help.

When Edgardo's father came to the school because Edgardo's coat was ripped, I felt like a shirker, because I couldn't do anything about it. He is a very young father who never went to school and he is terribly concerned for his son. He came to New York from Puerto Rico so his son could get an education and be with people who aspired to higher things. He doesn't want his son to be what *he* is. He wants his son to have a better life. It shows in the way he dresses his children that he doesn't want them to be considered slum children or lower class. He just wants them to be very Americanized—to be "real" Americans.

When you see this—when you see parents who almost get tears in their eyes when you say good things about their children, you almost haven't got the heart to sit there and say, "Well, now that I've told you all the good, let me tell you the bad." It may be that with some of the parents, I would get further by not mentioning the bad—by giving them something to be proud about. Maybe, when the parent goes home and says, "I got good news from the teacher," the child will feel that the teacher must really like him or she wouldn't have said good things to the parent. It could be.

That's one reason I would like to see Mrs. Thomas. I would like to tell her that I really like John Herbert. I think he's a fine person and has great potential. When I see that boy with his bright eyes and his energy, I want to do something for him even though I know he is very aggressive and has many destructive tendencies. For some reason, I seem to be able to work with him. He isn't like Eddy.

Maybe if I were able to tell his mother that John Herbert has a lot of good qualities, that he has the admiration of all the other boys in the class, that he is capable of swaying opinion one way or the other, she would begin to feel that he had some possibilities, too.

He really isn't unintelligent, even though he still can't read much. Every once in a while he surprises me with the things he notices. He saw the filmstrip of "Puss in Boots" and then said to me, "That wasn't no giant." I asked him what he meant and he said, "If the king and queen could sit in the giant's chair, it wasn't no giant." No one else in the class picked that out but he said that the story was ruined because it wasn't logical.

Another time, he was very critical of a filmstrip that was supposed to go along with a story in one of his books. He had looked through the book and read a little of it, but he was very disappointed in the filmstrip because it wasn't consistent with the book. He picked out all the little things that were wrong with it, things that I don't think I would ever have noticed.

I had a very interesting conversation with a social worker who went to John Herbert's home. She said that he was very hostile to her in school but that when she went to his home, he was a perfect host and was a completely different person. His mother quit her job because she apparently thinks that she should be with her boys more. However, the boys have a very bad relationship with their father. It won't matter if she quits twelve jobs and spends that much time with her children. They still don't have any identity with the father in the home.

I'd like to talk with her and completely surprise her by saying, "We all know that John Herbert has problems in school, but there are some things you may not have heard about him." Then, I would say two or three things that might really shock her to the place where she'd think, "Here is somebody who really *does* care about my son." I don't think it does any good to just "butter up" a parent, but if I could say that, in spite of the problems, these are some of the good things I want to talk about, it might do some good.

I remember once when I sent a "good note" home with Eddy, his mother started to swing at him before she read the note. She was so sure that it was for poor behavior that she didn't even bother to read it and it was a commendation note! It might be that this sort of thing should be sent through the mail. Someone like John Herbert, who can't read very well, would probably throw away anything a teacher gave him, because *he* would think it was bad.

You can't even let the children know you are sending anything if you use the mail. If you say that you are going to mail a letter to their parents, they will go home and open the mail boxes before their parents come home and take out anything they see that comes from the school. This is very widely known, and, in a way, you can't blame them. If I knew that I was going to get a beating because I was bad in school, I would do what I could to keep my mother from finding out. And I'm not a slum child.

There's no doubt that the positive approach can work if you know how to handle it. I finally achieved an orderly entrance to assembly that way, and we'd never had one before. I was determined to get order. I said, "When I walk down the hall, I want to walk as though I were alone on the street. There will be no one behind me. I'm not going to hear any noise and I'm not going to turn around. I'm not going to look around even once because I know there will be no one behind me." I repeated it all a few times and then I started to walk to the assembly—through the long hall, down the stairs, in the back door of the auditorium and down the center aisle. I walked all the way and there wasn't a sound. I walked on my toes and still didn't hear asound all the way down. I couldn't believe it. I didn't turn around once, and I usually have to stop about a dozen times and straighten them out.

It was dramatic and it was new, and there was an element of trust in it. If I had had to look around, it would have been like the story of Lot's wife. Everything would have been ruined. This isn't something that could be repeated every day. The thing is that with a group like this, you have to be continually creating gimmicks; you always have to be doing something different, and it wears you out.

I think that if I had started off at the beginning like that, I would now be able to handle the group better going downstairs. They would know what was expected of them and I wouldn't have any noise by now. Every day it's the same thing. We stop at the landing on the way down and three or four boys run off to the fountain for a drink of water. If I'm at the back of the line, I can stop them, but they run wildly down the stairs; if I'm at the front of the line I can control the speed but not the "runaways." It's one choice or the other, and for the children's safety I have chosen the front of the line. They are upset because the principal has met them on the stairs several times lately when they were misbehaving. That shock helps for a few days but *I'm* the one who has to take them down. I didn't start right and I didn't have any help in the beginning. Now I have to learn to do it myself.

I've had a real battle with hats, too. I asked them to take off their hats when they came into the room and never was I successful in getting them to do it. So I said, "I'll give you one warning each day. I'll allow you to forget once but after that, if I see a boy wearing a hat in the classroom, the hat

is mine until I think it's time to give it back." I collected a
lot of hats that way. When John Herbert was the one who
didn't take his off, he put up a big fight about giving it to me.
Then, when he finally gave it to me, one of the other boys
put his on and wouldn't give it up. I said, "We won't move
until you either give me the hat or go to see Mr. Morehouse
with me." Well, eventually he gave me the hat rather than
go to see the principal.

I get the feeling that these children are constantly testing you to see if you really mean to carry through on what
you say. If you tell them that you will warn them once and
punish them the next time, they will go ahead and do it anyway. When you punish them, most of them will accept it
gracefully, but a few will make a big fuss. Then, you have
to decide whether you are going to let them get away with
it or whether you are going to insist that they, just like everyone else, obey because they undermine the rest of the class.

I think that if I were to start with a group like this
again, I would start with a relatively few things that were
very important. I would forget about hats for awhile and
concentrate on the things that I must enforce at all costs.
Whatever else happens, these two or three things will be
the ones that are enforced. We *will* walk down the stairs in
an orderly way, for instance, because this is a dangerous
thing and involves other people. If I could narrow down the
area of conflict, I might be able to take a few things and not
have conflict all the time.

This means that I have to go through all the things that
bother me and pick out the ones that are most important.
That's very difficult. One of the things that annoys me more
than anything else is eating or chewing in class. They can't
speak because their mouths are full of bubble gum or candy.
They get the room in really terrible shape; their desks are
filled with candy wrappers and potato chips and all kinds
of garbage they bring in to eat. My classroom is always a
mess, and it gets on my nerves.

I can say a hundred times, "Anyone who has anything
in his mouth, throw it out now." I tell them that they have
three minutes to empty their mouths, and I won't even look
to see who does it. Then, after I have trusted them to get

rid of the food or gum, I see someone chewing again. It is like a game, and they try to see if they can't get in a fast chew once in awhile, without my seeing them. They tease me because they know it annoys me so much.

Next year, I am going to try to know what I expect when I come into the classroom. I didn't know what I could expect this year. It will help me set up more reasonable routines. But it won't do any good to read or talk about a lot of rules unless I can really get them into the habit of doing certain things in certain ways—unless I can make it an automatic thing. If I start the first day and say, "This is the way we go down the stairs," then, I must keep on doing it even if it takes a tremendous amount of time, and I am tired to death of working on it. If I can make the establishment of a few consistent routines the first most important thing of the year, more important than anything else, maybe I can get to real teaching and enjoying the class a whole lot sooner than I did this year.

Things didn't begin to get really organized until about April and I think that our assembly program helped a lot. I had put the program off until the last possible date because I didn't think I could handle it, but when the time came I had to plan something. I wanted something that wouldn't be too time-consuming in rehearsals, that wouldn't take too much time away from other classwork, and something that I could control.

I decided not to give a play. It would have been too hard with my group and, anyway, I was sick and tired of the kind of plays you usually see in assembly. They aren't for the children at all but are just ways for teachers to show off and get a lot of praise. No one expected my class to do anything decent. The only time we participated with the other groups, the assistant principal called on us last and acted like he was surprised that we did anything. I wasn't going to have my kids humiliated again if I could help it.

My mother, when she was teaching, had done a program with glass slides and she suggested that I try it. It happened to be very good because I saw that we could use it with our social studies unit. I really had to give it a build-up with the class. They wanted to act out a play, as the other groups had, but I made this idea sound like something very special. I showed them some slides that my mother's class had made, ten years ago, and told them how much better they could do. Finally, I got some glass for slides and the projector, which we were able to keep in the room all the time. This was a thrill.

It was a huge machine and nobody else in the school was allowed to touch it. It was our private property and the class looked on it as theirs. They were very concerned for fear the after-school-study-group which used our room would harm the machine. They even asked if we would have to pay for it if the other kids broke it; fortunately, nothing happened.

Little by little they got really enthusiastic. I wrote the dialogue and they made the slides. It was a slide program on how America began and every child had a chance to make a slide. As each slide was shown, a narrative was recited by an individual or a group of children. They got up together at the microphone and one would say one verse of a poem or a little speech. A group of the boys who didn't want to do the talking operated the machine.

I think the most enthusiastic person of all was John Herbert, who had the least to say. He introduced the program and closed it and adjusted the microphone for every person all the way through. He was not absent from one rehearsal or one performance. He was terrific!

The program went very smoothly, mainly because of the boys who ran the projector. They were shy; many of them were Puerto Rican and couldn't speak English very well; but they loved to work the machinery. They were so quick and worked together so well as a team. They learned everything about that machine. They even knew how to change the bulbs by the time they were finished.

The first time we gave the program, the loudspeaker wouldn't work and it went over very poorly. The fourth graders made so much noise they couldn't hear and no one paid any attention to the program. The children were very disappointed and they didn't want to do it for their own grade the next day, but I persuaded them to try again. It was a huge success with the fifth grade. Everything went smoothly, and the children were happy. The third time, the class got a little cocky and it wasn't quite as well done but the boys on the slide machine were the ones who made it. They were so quick. If anyone slipped up on a line and missed a cue, they just slid into the right place and put on the slide. I didn't even have to stand next to them or tell them anything. It was great.

John Herbert is a born leader, and he did all the little things that needed to be done; he took the program very seriously. For all his brashness, once he got up to that microphone to speak, he lowered his eyes and spoke very quietly. I was so proud of him.

The play helped a lot with other things, too. We decided to tape the dialogue and in order to do that we needed absolute quiet in the room. In the morning I wrote on the board, "Alphabetize the spelling words, divide them into syllables. Then, come to my desk, take a piece of paper, and answer the questions on your reading." All the time we were taping I didn't have to speak to anyone even once. They did everything in a very orderly way and when they handed in their papers, some of them even said, "Sorry, I didn't have time to finish." Other times they might say, "It's not done." But, here was a "sorry." It was a pleasure.

They like to have me make up arithmetic problems using their kind of names. If I give them a problem about Steve or Bill, they can't read it, but they *can* read their own names. Sometimes the situation is so ludicrous they begin to laugh. I might say that Jose and Manuel went fishing in a lake, when they have never really seen a lake or been near a fishhook. They feel so personally involved and it shows that you are thinking about them, too.

I did start something else about that time that also worked out well. I began to teach arithmetic by using colored disks. I had had the disks from the beginning of the year but Mrs. James, the math coordinator, told me not to use them because the kids would throw them around like paper airplanes. Well, when we go to working on multiplication, I decided to use them anyway. I gave each child a long envelope with a cord closing and I had them put their names on their own envelopes. Then, I let each child come up to my desk and pick out eighteen disks. I watched how they were counting. Some, counted by twos, some by threes, and some by ones.

Not a child threw them around. The most difficult children in the room were the first ones to get their disks arranged as I asked them. One boy who has done nothing all year fixed his disks on his desk. It has been tremendously successful because we are flying through simple multiplication, now. I collect the envelopes, keep them in my desk and give them out every day. The children have shown self-control by using them correctly.

We did something else along that line, too. Each child made nine cards and then wrote the numbers 2, 4, 6, 8, up to 18—one number on each card. When I said, "Three 2's," they held up the card that showed the answer. I thought it would be chaos, but they could play it for ten hours and not get bored. There is no talking, no yelling out—they just hold up cards. I have to put my glasses on because I can't see to the back of the room without them. They think that's very funny. Really, it moves them along. In two days they learned all the 2's and there is no trouble at all.

My children are reading a lot more, too, but I can't say that all of it shows up on the tests. I think it's more the interest and the ability to figure out a new word that's different now. They are slow, but they can concentrate, and they can use syllables and phonics to find out how words are pronounced. Of course, they still need a lot of help because often they don't know what words mean and, if they can't comprehend, they're not reading.

I wish that next year I could have a test given near the beginning of the year, in September or October, and have the results right away. If they were really good tests they would at least tell me where to begin. Then I could give the tests again to find out how much progress we were making.

Three of the kids I have this year are going to be in the highest group next year. They have really shown a tremendous amount of interest and they should be able to do it. About fifteen will be in the lowest sixth grade and they will have a very good teacher. No one was held back because most

of them have missed a grade before. Some of them will probably have to repeat the sixth grade because they won't be able
to make high enough scores on the reading test even if they
do gain a lot.

I guess I'm the one who has learned the most. I don't
think I could go through another year like this one. Even if
I have another slow class I won't let them get out of hand like
I did this year. I had the wrong idea of friendliness first and
firmness last. Now, I really love this group of kids. I know
I'm going to miss them when they leave my room.

I have written a story for them about a teacher who
comes to a new school and before she meets her class for the
first time she tries to decide what each child may be like. Of
course, the story's teacher was really me and each imaginary
child was one of my own. I put in a description of *every* child
in the room and no one seemed displeased by what I said about
him. For every fault I mentioned, there was something good.
I had done this for the group I had had in student teaching,
and the reaction was exactly the same. They made me read it
over twice; they liked it. It made me feel that maybe an ounce
of success had been attained. They sat still, they listened,
and they enjoyed it, too!

I was exhausted by this first year but toward the end I
began to feel that I was planning much more realistically for
their needs. I left much more time for discussion and for
interpretation. I planned fewer things and went a little bit
slower and brought my expectations nearer to what my children were able to do.

I am sure that this year has been tremendous training
for any other, because it will never be as hard again. I know
now that even though another class may be a little more
academically oriented, they will need to have just as much
careful planning done for them. The slower class may need
more time, but the faster children will need the same amount
of interest shown in them. I think I could teach anywhere
after this year.

I sometimes wonder how I managed to stick it out. When
people say, "Why are you teaching in such a terrible neighborhood?", I have to say that I chose it. Then, when they ask

me if I like it, I have to stop and think. If I say that I don't
like it, I will be admitting to myself that I made a wrong
choice—that I'm in the wrong field. I can't do that. I made
my choice and I'm going to stick it out.

Of course, I have had a lot of help from my parents, from
other teachers, and from the group of Teaching Corps students who have met together this year. I had help, too, from
our teacher-trainer coordinator—mostly encouragement,
rather than specific suggestions of what to do. It was just
good to know that she felt I was there doing a job and that she
believed I could do it. She was proud of us. The school had
never had student teachers who wanted to come back to teach
there, and she felt that this was adding to the atmosphere
of the school. Some of the other teachers are really terrific
people. They will surely be outstanding educators in the
future; they will do—and have done—a lot for children.

I'm glad I stuck it through. I'm very proud that I'm
going back to the same school next year. I feel that if I take
something on, no matter how hard it is, I've got to see it
through to the end. I guess it all adds up to one thing. People expected a lot of me and I tried to live up to their
expectations.

5

"I've learned a lot this year . . .

. . . but two things stand
out. I like to call them
my two keys to teaching in
depressed-area schools. The
first is anticipation of
what is going to happen. . . .
Another thing . . . is consistency of thought, of action, and of feeling for the
children. . . . It is through
anticipation and consistency
that I feel a teacher in a
depressed area can make the
greatest progress in helping
these children to learn to
live with each other and to
respect themselves and other
people as much as possible."

During most of my high school career, I was mainly interested in athletics and not so much in the academic part of school. I went out for the swimming, golf, and basketball teams, and I never actually concentrated on any of my studies. Therefore, my report cards usually said that I had a good mind, and a good potential, but I never seemed to settle down and work hard in order to become a consistent student. It was sometime during my senior year in high school that a change came over me; I became interested in the academic along with the athletic. I decided it wasn't enough to go through high school and cram for the tests and make my 85, 88, or 90 grades; I realized that, in order to enter a fairly good college, I would have to buckle down and do some work. So, during the first semester of my senior year, I consistently put in about two hours a day at studying, in addition to the time I spent at athletics, and I came out with an A average. I believe this had a great deal to do with getting into the college I wanted, although it did not bring up my whole grade average to any considerable degree.

I had always planned to go to college—in our family it was just taken for granted that my sister and I would go. From the time I began to earn money, half of it was always banked especially for my education.

We were never really a wealthy family, so during the summers it was easier on my parents for my sister and me to earn our own money. I ran a summer swimming camp for three years when I was in high school. I began teaching swimming when I was about ten years old. I swam for a competitive swimming team where all the members taught other children who went to a public school day camp. But, since my grandfather had a swimming pool, I thought I might as well get paid for teaching, so I went into business for myself. When I was in ninth grade, I went into partnership with a tenth-grade girl and we made about $800 that summer working every day from nine in the morning to four in the afternoon. We charged a dollar a lesson.

The second year, I started giving each child three lessons a week for a flat five dollars, cutting down my teaching to Mondays, Wednesdays, and Fridays. I employed a girl to teach with me for ten hours a week and, after paying her salary, I banked about 75 per cent of the profit. From the very first I banked all of this in order to buy clothes, to help pay for golf and other sports I was interested in; but one half was especially saved for college.

Throughout my high school life, in fact throughout my whole life, my family was always interested in physical activity and in an intellectual life as well. As far back as I can remember we always had a great variety of people in the house. My parents associated with the leading artists, writers, journalists, etc., in our city. They were friendly with musicians, people around the neighborhood, people in Red Cross, people in education. They were concerned with such things as the Experiment in International Living, juvenile delinquency, and racial integration. In other words, I enjoyed a home of great diversity and great stimulation.

During my senior year at high school I started applying to different colleges. I applied to Kendall, to a very fine school near my home, and to several others. I applied to Kendall because of my diving coach who had gone to school up there, and who had recommended it as a very fine school for swimming and for academic studies as well. After sending out all my applications and meeting people from all the schools, I picked Kendall. I usually pick a place, when everything else seems to be equal, on the type of people who are in charge. I thought the people at Kendall would fulfill their promise that scholastics and an education would come first.

This proved to be true in my senior year, when I had to drop out of one of the most important swimming meets because of the thesis I was writing. In fact, the swimming coach—who was also dean of students—put it on the line: if I went to the meet and dived, we had a chance of winning; if I did not go, he did not see that we had any chance at all. Then he said, "But it's your decision to make." I told him after thinking about it for a couple of days, that I had to finish the thesis and would have to bow out of the meet. I did, and he never held a grudge. Of course, we won—and that helped.

During this whole time, I was fairly confident I would either go into the real estate business with my father or into something like psychology or law. I don't think my father and I actually sat down and talked about it; it was more or less understood. If I wanted to come in with him, I would be able to, and he would welcome me. He would also understand if I wanted to do something else. I wouldn't have to make up any pretenses. I could just go in and tell him I wasn't interested in real estate. We have always had this kind of free-flowing type of communication.

However, there was a tremendous amount of academic pressure at Kendall, and about the middle of my junior year I started realizing that I really didn't want business, law, or psychology. I wanted to go into one of the academic fields and I wanted to teach.

It is hard to explain the academic pressure at Kendall but it made it seem that being confronted by and wrestling with various ideas was a much greater challenge than wrestling with a physical opponent. In other words, scholastic achievement was constantly played up at Kendall while athletics were constantly submerged. There was a tremendous academic undercurrent, all focussing upon the ultimate entrance into a graduate school. It almost got to the point where just to graduate was nothing if you were not admitted to graduate school.

It's a little hard to remember when I started becoming interested in education. Sometime in my junior year I decided I wanted to go to graduate school, get a master's degree in English, then a doctorate, and then probably go into teaching on the college level. Sometime later, however, my roommate, Jack, told me about a very interesting possibility. If I wanted to make money while I was earning my doctorate, I could first become certified to teach English in high school and support myself while finishing my doctor's degree. He knew these things because his father was in education; Jack too, was expecting to teach. Jack set up interviews for me in a couple of schools but at Teachers College he arranged for me to talk to the coordinator of the program in elementary education instead of in English.

I realized at the beginning of the interview that I had been tricked, but I thought if Jack had gone this far I might as well do him the courtesy of finding out what the program in elementary education was all about. I came away from the interview without any decision as to what I would do.

I finally made up my mind to go into the Teachers College elementary education program on the basis of my interview and because of my interest in children and my work with them since the ninth grade. I believe the fact that my roommate was going to be in the same program had some influence too.

I remember that, when I went back to Kendall and announced to the chairman of the English department that I was going into elementary education, this caused quite a stir. I had a hard time convincing them that this was what I wanted to do. Even then I don't feel I was fully convinced myself. It wasn't until I was student teaching, working with depressed-area children, that I really became committed and enthusiastic about teaching as an intellectual challenge.

Everyone in the English department at Kendall said elementary education would be a humdrum, deadening type of existence and a boring type of teaching, but I found it just the opposite. I think now, more than ever, I could say to them that they wouldn't have the type of student they have at Kendall if it weren't for the elementary school teachers in the student's life who had asked a few questions and had given the child the basic skill to go ahead and ask his own questions. I no longer need to feel defensive about being an elementary school teacher. It's not anti-intellectual; it's tremendously challenging.

However, the first semester experiences at Teachers College were somewhat disappointing. I found intellectual stimulation among the students, since they were generally of good calibre, but the work was different from what I had experienced at Kendall. I finally did realize, after the first weeks, that this program was preparing me to teach, and that I had to start with many basic things of a pragmatic nature.

The overriding experience the first semester was in the sixth grade—a very, very low sixth-grade class. Interestingly enough, the cooperating teacher and I had the same basic philosophic approach and ideas about education. We both believed that each child has a potential and that he has a right to develop his potential as much as possible. We also believed it was our responsibility to create a learning environment for the children so that they could develop their potential and find some sort of order of existence for themselves. This environment should be based upon the ability of the children to think critically and analytically about the world around them and the larger questions of life. I feel this teacher was very good. She had a tremendous amount of warmth, sincerity, and compassion for the children.

During my second semester at Teachers College, I was in a pilot project. I joined the project for two basic reasons. One was that I felt it was an honor to be asked; only seven out of the seventy students in the whole program were selected. The other, which was the main reason, was just the outright challenge of the whole affair. The idea of working in a depressed area, trying to make some headway with these children, and trying to become a better teacher appealed to me greatly.

I had already had some experience with depressed-area children in the early part of my life at home. My parents were very interested in camping and in work with juvenile delinquents. The camp I attended as a camper and as a junior counselor was run for handicapped children. My father was a member of the board of directors. This camp had a very interesting idea about handicapped children. They applied the term "handicapped" not only to children who were born with physical defects or who were deaf or blind, but also to children who came from very low socio-economic backgrounds. So the camp included children who could not take advantage of the usual camping programs because of physical *or* financial lacks.

My parents were also interested in work with juvenile delinquents and with racial integration. I sometimes shared my room at home with boys who had gotten into trouble and were being helped by my father. Thus I had a good background for the interest which developed during my student teaching.

The whole program during the second semester was a generally positive one. We had excellent cooperating teachers; I know that my teacher was one of the best I have ever encountered in any school. I also think that the way she let me begin my teaching was truly worthwhile.

I remember her asking me, when I first came into the situation, if I wanted to begin teaching right away. I told her I was more interested at first in watching the classroom, letting the children get to know me and establishing some kind of rapport and consistency before actually teaching. I did this for about a week and a half to two weeks. At the end of two weeks I started my teaching in math as my cooperating teacher requested, and soon I was able to take over the whole class. I know that other student teachers began teaching right away; however, I don't believe any of them took over the whole class any sooner than I did.

By the end of the year, my cooperating teacher and I were running a modified team-teaching project in which I was teaching the math, social studies, and a little bit of science each day, and she was teaching reading and music and art. We collaborated on teaching gym and health. I am sure it was a very effective way of learning to become a good teacher.

I also think the fact that our cooperating teachers had regular class sessions each week with the coordinator of the Teachers College program was an important part of our project. The feedback from the teachers' group to us was highly important for our growth. Our work with the community was not that strong a part of our program. I would have liked to have participated in more lectures and more conferences and seen more projects and things which were going on in the community. I think one major problem was a lack of communication. For the most part, however, the experiences that we did have were very valuable. I think all of us benefitted.

Probably the most positive experience of our project was the written report which we prepared at the end of the semester on the preparation of teachers for service in depressed urban areas. This caused us to do more reading, more thinking about what we were reading and what we had observed; it also pulled us together in a more understanding seminar. I don't think any seminar I have ever been in has had such solidarity as this one.

As the end of the term drew nearer, it was time for me to decide where I wanted to teach. At first, I thought I would like to go to another country or another part of the United States. However, several things changed my mind. Those of us who had been in the special project were offered a chance to continue to work as a group during the next year with the coordinator of the program. I was also interested in getting my doctorate in the language arts area with a professor with with whom I had been working, and I knew that in two or three years I would have a good chance of being chosen as an instructor in the preservice program from which I graduated. Therefore, I decided to continue in the same school for my first year of teaching.

I feel that I am in a very well-run school; it is well-organized and is a place where new approaches and new ideas are welcomed, not only by the administration, but by the faculty as well. The principal is a wise and intellectual person. I am also impressed by the great degree of enthusiasm and respect shown to the assistant principal, who is often the disciplinarian and who does the little things that make the school run well.

The faculty seems very compatible with an interesting flow of ideas from one to another. There is also a great deal of encouragement from the administration for trying new ideas. In the sixth grade, they have team teaching. In the other grades there is a class which is a mixture of third and fourth graders, a kind of ungraded class. There is great emphasis on the kindergarten, on language arts, and on keeping the class groups small. Generally, throughout the whole school, new ideas are constantly being tried, whether they are in math, reading or anything else.

I began, in September, teaching fourth graders in a 4-4 class. This was considered a low class, since there were only five sections in the fourth grade. I taught this class until January, when I was asked to go up into the sixth grade and take over a team-teaching situation.

My fourth-grade class had eleven boys and nine girls; ten were holdovers, and five were guidance cases. This meant that I had ten children who should have been in the fifth grade, but—because of reading retardation—they were in the fourth grade for a second time. Five of the group had case records in the guidance office and were known to be problem children throughout the school.

It is difficult to know where to begin in describing my experiences in the fourth grade. I think I should first state the four principles that I believe to be of utmost importance for a classroom situation of this kind in a depressed area. I heard these first in a lecture by Ruth Levitos of the Department of Psychiatry of the New York Medical College. I have elaborated upon them, and they have been very important in my thinking ever since. The first principle is to provide for as much gratification as possible within each child. Then it is important to avoid frustration and to avoid aggression and violence in the classroom. And the fourth is to provide for a consistent ego development within each child. I don't believe that any of these can be accomplished separately; rather, the teacher must take all four and blend them together to get the best possible working situation. Perhaps the following example best illustrates these four points.

When our children come into the school situation, they lack many abilities and skills that a middle-class child has normally acquired at home. These depressed-area children have very poor auditory and visual discrimination. Martin Deutsch has written that depressed area children have little general conversation directed toward them in the home. They are constantly told to do this or don't do that, and they rarely come in contact with just normal conversation directed toward them to which they are expected to respond. There is also a lack of reading materials in these homes and the child does not develop an interest in learning to read before he comes to school.

When these children come to kindergarten and first or second grade, they are confronted with a tremendous amount of reading material, many rules and regulations, and a lot of talk. So far as these children are concerned, this might as well be in a foreign language. The Puerto Rican child has grown up in a home with a Spanish background and the Negro child, especially if he is an in-migrant from the South. speaks what is almost a different language in contrast to the English he encounters in school. All these things help to create a frustrating situation for the child, because he is not able to succeed in doing the things that are expected of him.

When my children came to the fourth grade after having been held back a year, which was frustrating and broke down their concepts of themselves as acceptable people, they were ten or eleven years old instead of the normal eight or nine. They had already become accustomed to the fact that they were going to fail again. If, in the beginning, I had demanded a great amount of reading, neatness, and exactness in everything the child did, I would have created another frustrating experience for the child.

In this environment, and with this frustration, a child can find little gratification in a school situation. At the same time, this frustration has to be let out somewhere, and often it is expressed in violence and aggression toward other children in the class, toward the teacher, and toward the school in general. When this happens the teacher has to step in and discipline the child, which, in turn, continues to break down the child's self respect, just as it has been broken down step-by-step in his earlier school experiences. This whole thing becomes a very invidious situation and creates its own vicious circle.

Therefore, basing my teaching on these four principles —providing gratification for each child, providing for ego development, avoiding violence and aggression, and avoiding frustration—I set up my class. The first day I stated what I expected of each child. I defined my limits and my rules as explicitly as possible, and yet I used the minimum number of rules. I felt—and I have continued to feel—that good discipline is a matter of demanding and receiving attention when you want it. It rather hinges on the fact that you must be discriminating in the routines that you set up. In other words, if you set up too many rules, and if you try to define too many limitations for the children, then you are obliged to consistently enforce them. If you fail you will probably lose control of the class, or at least you will put yourself back so far that it will be very hard to acquire a good, firm grip on the class again.

I walked in the first day and said, "I don't know what your other teachers have told you, and I am new to this school, so I don't know what you have done in the past. But I know the way I want you to line up, I know the way I want you to walk down the stairs, and I know the way I want you to behave in class. So that is the way we are going to do it." And then I proceeded to go through with it.

For example, in walking downstairs I lined them up in size places with the smallest children at the beginning and the tallest child at the end of the line. These children liked the security of having a place that belonged to them alone because they didn't have much of their own in their crowded living conditions. I then appointed two leaders and told the whole group about the basic rule of the school concerning running—the dangers of running—and good safety habits in walking down the stairs. I reminded them that too much noise would disturb other classes. We practiced walking up and down the steps the first day with their going only the number of steps that I told them to go. If we were on the fourth floor I would say, "Go down to the landing between the third and fourth floors and wait." They would go down one flight of stairs and wait. When everybody assembled there and was quiet, I would say, "All right, now go down to the next landing." After a week of stopping them at every landing and holding them until they were quiet, I was able to say, "Go out the door and down to the third floor landing and wait for me." This meant that they could take two flights of stairs. In this way, we set up routines.

The basic rule was that, at all times, respect and courtesy should be shown for every individual in the classroom. It meant that what they would like done for them in the classroom they must do for the others and for me. We talked about this awhile, and they seemed to understand it. Then I said, "All right. When you want to speak raise your hand and I'll listen to you and I won't turn my back on you and we'll all be quiet. And when I'm speaking, you will all listen to me and watch me. I will give you three warnings and after the third warning I will severely punish you." And this is what I did.

The very first day one of the little boys started rolling his pencils on his desk and not paying attention. It wasn't so much that he was actually being bad. Later, I found out that he didn't have very much intellectual ability, but I didn't know this at the time, so when it happened I had to deal with it as though he were confronting me—not necessarily me, but confronting authority. He rolled his pencils three or four times and I said, "I'm talking, and when you roll your pencils you prevent Rosemary from listening to me. You prevent Doris from listening, and you're not listening either. That means three people. Now if you don't want to listen to me Roger, that's your business, but don't roll your pencils as that means that two other people who sit near you can't listen."

He did it again about fifteen minutes later during a math period when I was explaining something on the board. I said, "You have had two warnings. The next time I am going to punish you." He was all right for about fifteen or twenty minutes. Other people were talking and we had done other things. But I had made a threat that I would have to carry out.

Sure enough, he did roll them again—whether he forgot or whether he was testing me or what have you—and I had to do what I said I would do. I took his pencils away and broke them and had him stand in a corner. This was the first

day and I was new and they were new and I was determined
to set up the classroom and go in there and be the boss. This
was actually the first confrontation.

I had really prepared for that first day. I went through
all the records and I put each child in a seat where I wanted
him to sit. I went according to what other teachers had said.
If three or four teachers said, "Unsatisfactory behavior in
class," I took this to mean that the child was a potential
trouble maker. It didn't necessarily mean he would get into
trouble with me, but I was taking no chances, so I put him
near the other children who had good reports. I separated
boys and girls and I tried to isolate the trouble-makers
around the room. This boy happened to be the first one who
did anything, so I stationed myself near him. I had planned
that if anything happened I would deal with it right away.
When this boy continued to roll his pencils—it's a petty thing
but it could set the tone for the whole year—I stationed myself so that I wasn't too far away to get over to him. That
way I could act immediately when I had to.

I think that we should realize these children come from
a different environment and background. They have little
opportunity to express themselves in their homes and for
the most part from what I've read and what I've personally
observed from being in the homes, they are physically punished quite severely for minute things. If they come into the
classroom the first day and the rules and limits are defined
for them and they overstep, then they know that they have
done something wrong. And if I, as a teacher, try and reason with them and say, "Now look, this isn't the right way
to behave" and do all this in terms of reasoning and rational
explanation, they will just tab me as being weak, soft, and
not consistent.

It wouldn't help anyway, because eventually I would ex-
plode and do something harsh and out of line with the image
I had been trying to construct in the classroom. Then I would
really be termed unfair by the children. It would be a valid
judgment on the children's part based on what they had been
able to see and encounter in the classroom. So I feel a teacher
should be "tough"—not in the physical sense, but very firm

—and give his warnings and make sure the children know it. Then he has to enforce those rules. Making a child, for a small misdemeanor, stand in a corner for half an hour or so as punishment should make the others wonder what will happen if they do something really out of line. At any rate, I suppose that this is the sort of thinking that would occur.

The whole area of courtesy was very important to me with these children in the 4-4 class. I tried always to be consistent in insisting that they show respect and courtesy toward their fellow students. Everyone had a chance to talk, and the other people sat and listened instead of trying to break in and interrupt. They also had to keep their hands to themselves and not push or shove, because they wouldn't want it done to them. One of the main ways of showing respect for each other, however, was not laughing when someone made a mistake. They learned to realize that everybody had something to offer in the classroom but everybody would make mistakes and we should respect each other and help one another.

I don't think that courtesy and respect in a classroom can be achieved without the teacher also being courteous and respectful to the children. I can't ever remember walking out of the room ahead of the girls, unless it was for a specific reason, such as if one of the boys had left and I had to stop him, or if I had to lead the group to some special place. But usually I would open the doors for the children or if one dropped his pencil on the floor and I happened to be standing by, I'd pick it up for him. And I never would ask them to do anything that I wouldn't do myself.

After I had the room pretty well set up and things were going smoothly most of the time, I was told that I was going to get a girl who had had to leave two other schools and who had spent six months at City Hospital in the children's ward. She was considered quite emotionally disturbed, an older girl who should have been in the sixth grade. I put some responsibility on the children by telling them that we were going to have a new child in the classroom, and she had been sick for awhile and might be quite nervous. I didn't go into a lot of detail, but I tried to give them just enough information so they would get the idea this was someone they would have to understand. She hadn't been well, and we would have to be responsible for her. The girl came into the classroom and the children reacted very favorably. They were quite responsible and understood what I had told them. I had also told them that I would overlook some things that she did and they would just have to understand that everybody is different—everyone has his own problems—and they would be expected to maintain very high standards while this new girl was getting used to the class.

The first day—I remember it was during an art period, and I had only six children in the classroom—we had our first difficulty. She had spent a fairly good day and was quiet. She was on sedatives three times a day. I said, "Let's all sit the correct way so we can get ready to go," but she continued to kneel in her chair instead of sitting up ready to go. I said, "You know how to sit right—as a young lady should—and we are not going to be able to leave until you sit correctly. I am sure that your neighbor doesn't want you putting your hands all over her and whispering in her ear. Let's sit up and get ready to go." Very reluctantly she did. I erased something from the board, and turned around to see her making obscene gestures behind my back. This quite shocked the two little girls in the classroom, because no one had ever done this to me before.

I tried to control myself, but this is a rude thing and it challenges your authority all down the line. Finally I walked over to her and very slowly and solemnly with everyone watching me to see what I would do, I said, "In this classroom we show respect for one another. You weren't being very respectful by kneeling in your chair, you were holding up everyone in the classroom. And then to do something like this—I don't want to see anything like this ever again, and if you do it you will be punished. You are new in the classroom and I'll give you a warning. If you are going to act like a baby, you will be treated like a baby, and this sort of thing is very childish. You embarrass yourself in front of the other people here. I know that Rosemary and Gloria are very embarrassed that you would do something like that."

I don't know whether it registered. There was a kind

of blank look on her face as she gazed back at me. But she never did that again as far as I know.

This girl did cause trouble and bully other children, but for the most part she seemed to be able to adjust fairly well to the particular class situation that we had. I visited her two or three times at City Hospital, when she returned there for checkups and I also visited her at her home. I noticed that after each visit her behavior in class grew markedly better and more consistently normal. For the time that she was in our class she was generally able to fit in and to function.

You can't rule by force, unless you want to be mean to all the children. You can rule with meanness, but I would say this is absolutely out. In order to establish discipline in a class so that eventually you will be able to teach, you have to set up routines in the beginning and everlastingly enforce them. Mostly it is just repetition. It is not any kind of harsh discipline or taking away of privileges. It is just repetition over and over again. It is establishing yourself as an authority figure who knows what he wants and intends to have it that way. It is just constantly saying the same things over and over again.

It can become a very demoralizing thing, and I know it drains you physically, to keep repeating something; usually it boils down to the same four or five children that you have to speak to, and that is something that just has to be accepted. There will be days when you will let down a little bit, but you must be consistent as much as you can. A lot of it is based on just dull repetition for yourself and for the children. You have to do this with them. Eventually they learn.

Near the end of September or early in October, I realized that teaching in a whole-class situation was another source of frustration for these children, especially since there were so many individual differences. Although all the children had approximately a beginning second-grade reading ability, and could therefore be considered to be homogeneously grouped according to reading ability, this did not hold true for all the other things they were expected to do in a classroom situation. Therefore, I began doing extensive grouping about the first part of October.

To begin I gave a series of tests—teacher-made tests— in spelling, mathematics, reading, and social studies. Then I went home, studied all of these, and broke the children into groups in reading, mathematics and spelling based on ability. In social studies I decided to organize the groups on the bases of ability and work habits—that is, ability to work with other children, personality, etc. Generally the ones that were strong in reading were the better students all around. So they became the leaders in the social studies group.

I didn't start all these groups at once, but I worked up to it gradually. In order to provide for as much success as possible at first, I picked a very easy subject. I assigned five of the better students to write up reports about a fish tank and a turtle tank and some plants we had in the room. I let this group go back in the corner and work by themselves on their reports. There were one or two weak ones in the group, but they got extra help from the others and so did not feel they were losing out and did not become frustrated. I tried to set up the group so that they would not become disinterested or bored and start acting up in the back of the room while I was teaching something else up at the front.

The children worked well together. They did not seem frustrated. They wrote some very good reports and mounted them for display purposes. I believe it helped their self-respect to have their names put on the displays, which were set up around the fish tanks where all the teachers, the principal, and the other children could see them.

The next type of group work involved a little larger group with one or two children doing the actual leading. Again, I had a very simple project that involved all the children so that each felt he had accomplished something. I didn't want them to be frustrated or disappointed at the end.

After the children sensed what I was looking for and what I was trying to do, I moved to much more involved grouping based on the tests I had given. The actual beginning of this grouping was preceded by a discussion session in which I tried to explain exactly why we were doing this.

I explained to them very frankly and honestly that not all children in the room learned the same thing at the same time, and that it was silly for those who were ready to learn multiplying to have to keep on adding and subtracting with the others. This was boring for them. But, I said, the people who could multiply might not be able to read very well, and it was ridiculous for other people to read very simple stories when they could be reading harder ones. I then explained that we would break up into groups so that everyone could read, or do arithmetic, or science, or anything else at their own speed. I emphasized repeatedly that this did not mean that one person was necessarily smarter than another, but that, just as some people could run very fast, often a person who could not run very fast might be able to do mathematics very quickly. I believe they understood this.

I organized three large groups in math, three large groups in spelling, five groups of four children each in social studies, and four groups of four, five, or six—depending upon the ability of the children—in reading. There were three math groups in the beginning but depending upon the type of work they were doing, they could easily be broken down into subgroups. By the end of my time with them, they had become very sophisticated about being able to work in, for example, Group A—a large group, knowing that, after they had completed a certain number of problems, they would join small subgroup A-1 or eventually work with another subgroup on flash cards with multiplication facts or something else.

By the middle of October I had this going well enough so I could come into the class and start a typical day that would be something like the following:

At nine o'clock after taking attendance and after collecting milk money, lunch money, trip money, bank money, and just money money, I would give about five minutes of dictation to increase their auditory ability. At the end of the dictation, I would either give a spelling pretest or an actual spelling test. This was done for three groups and I would say, "Group One word," and give the word and a sentence. Then I would give a Group Two word and a Group Three word. After the spelling test, I would tell the children that we had certain things to do in mathematics. For example, we had to work on the idea of sets in our multiplication facts. I would tell Group A that it was going to work on 7's, 8's, and 9's, while Groups B and C were going to be working on the 5's, 10's, and 2's.

I would also tell them that we had a certain amount of work we wanted to do in social studies concerning the painting of our murals and constructing our puppets or the making of a class newspaper. If we had to do two stories in the basal reader, I would tell the class that there would be an hour for library period sometime during the day. This was not really cooperative planning, but it could have developed into something like that if I had had a longer time with this group. As it was, they understood what we were going to do, and why, before we began work.

I'd then say that we would like to start working with Group A in mathematics and while we were doing this Group One in reading and Group Three in social studies would begin work in their particular areas. Each group had a special place where they were supposed to work and the children in each group moved to the same area each time. Then I would say, "Reading Group One, move to your place; Group Three of social studies, move to your place; the rest of you come to the front of the room to work with me."

When I had a social studies group and a math group working at the same time, I checked it out pretty carefully the night before to be sure no one from the social studies group was in the math group with which I wanted to work. Quite often, all the social studies groups would work at one time, although one group might finish sooner than the others. When that happened they understood they were to go on to another part of the curriculum: multiplication facts, spelling, or something we had already worked out.

Many times I would start with the math group and assign the reading material that I wanted the other children to do with the questions either mimeographed on a sheet or written on the board. I had already set the routines of how I wanted the questions answered and everything. I would have an original group of maybe six in the slow reading group, and I would have eight in the top math group. If a boy was very good in math but very poor in reading, this meant he could do some math on his own, but would have to work with me in the reading class. Thus, he could—in math —work towards independence, while still receiving individual help in the other subject. But this didn't happen very often.

With twenty children I could do this grouping, although it was potentially quite a volcanic little group. There were times when I had individual conferences with children on their reading. Some days I would notice that the whole group was really reading quite steadily. This would appear to be a day when they were going to be able to sit, as a whole group, so I would just kind of throw the math out of the window for that particular morning. I would just let the reading go on as long as it seemed to be working—a sort of saturation process.

Then there were days when I had to juggle groups and move very quickly from one thing to another. It depended on how they reacted the first hour or so of the day. This sounds a little hectic and as if there wasn't very much super- vision, but during the math times I would be constantly cir- cling the room, asking questions and breaking down the math groups into smaller subgroups so that each child was giving another child problems. This would, at the same time, allow me to observe what was going on in the back of the room and keep an eye on specific children. The children also knew that if they had a question they could raise their hands and we would stop and quickly answer the question. If the ques- tion were too involved I would have to ask the child to wait for a few minutes until I had a chance to get back there to answer it.

It had its shortcomings. Naturally some of the children were left out; but for the most part each child had a sense of doing individual work and a sense of importance and indi- viduality in school. They weren't all expected to do the same thing at the same time in the same way.

I believe that my group work was successful because I had a discipline of a sort that enabled me to get a child back in his seat with a snap of my fingers, even if I was across the room. Nine times out of ten it would work. Sometimes it took a second warning.

This sort of control was successful because the children understood there were specific times throughout the day when they could have free time to talk and play some games or anything else they enjoyed. I was not a stickler for perfect silence in the classroom. They thought at first that I was being lax or weak about it. But they soon learned that I would stop any talking that did not have something to do with schoolwork. If a child was asking a question or talking about something that had to do specifically with what he was doing at the time or something that would be involving him later, I usually let it go and passed over it. Again the success here rests on the teacher's consistency in continually backing this up and not becoming so worn out or frustrated that he jumps on some child who *is* talking about schoolwork. The teacher, if he is going to follow this plan, must always try to let the children talk about schoolwork and not stop them. If he wants to stop talking altogether, then this must be done as efficiently as possible and must be done with the children realizing fully and exactly what you are asking for and why you are doing it.

Working with this fourth grade, I was not so overtly concerned with actual factual content such as "Christopher Columbus did not actually step on the mainland of North America—true or false" as some teachers were. I was more interested in the children learning how to work together in intimate little groups with as much skill as possible. I won't ever know whether I was completely successful—not completely successful, that would be hard to say—whether I was successful at all with any of the children, since I was taken out after four and a half months with the class.

However, none of the children, while they were with me, were ever sent down to the guidance office, and none of the mothers had to come in. Also, a short test of my own showed that the average reading ability for the whole class, after the time I had them, was 2.8 which was an average gain of six months. A few of them gained much more.

These children had come to see themselves as one of the best classes on the fourth-grade level, since they were the only class that consistently gave demonstration lessons for other teachers, for student teachers and for "visiting firemen." They were also asked to give an assembly presentation for not only the fourth grade but for the fifth and sixth grades.

There was some sort of ego development and success feeling within all these children; but as to actual knowledge of my ultimate success, that was ended on the last day of January when I was with the class for the last time.

I found out, through the grapevine, that I would probably be asked to move to the sixth grade because two sixth grade teachers were leaving. About a month later, the principal talked to me after a faculty meeting and asked me how I would feel about moving from my 4-4 class to the 6-1 class and into a team teaching situation. At the time he asked me to think about it and come back in a couple of days with an answer. Right then I knew I didn't need to wait a couple of days. I told him I did not think it would be the right thing for my 4-4 class—that possibly it would be highly demoralizing for them and would not be a good move at all. But he said to take some more time and think about it.

About a week later I wrote him a letter stating that these children were termed underachievers and slow learners. They had a very low average IQ, they were mostly from minority groups, and, in other years, they had had very poor attendance records. For the past four months they had one of the finest attendance records in the school, none of them had to go to the guidance counselor, and as a whole class they were able to get along with each other and with the rest of the children in the school. They had come to have a very good feeling about themselves and I felt that if I was pulled out of the class it would reinforce everything detrimental they had learned before in their environment and in the school situation—that is, not only were they the ones on the bottom of the ladder, with whom nothing good stayed for very long, but also they were looked down upon and no one really cared about them. I said that at this point they had finally come to have some kind of feeling among themselves. They had potential, and they were individuals. It wasn't that no other teacher could do the job, but, being realistic, there was a high degree of rapport among all of us in the classroom. Any other teacher would be coming in with a real handicap, and it wouldn't be the best thing for the group.

The principal took the letter and wrote me a nice answer, but said he wished I would still think about it because he was having trouble getting another sixth-grade teacher of the calibre he wanted. He said I should continue thinking, but that he would take under advisement everything I had said. A few day later he called me again and asked me if I had changed my mind. By this time, I didn't like all this responsibility being put on me when I was the teacher and he was the principal. Also, I didn't want to cross him that much; it would just be bad politics. So I said my feelings remained the same, that I was still completely opposed to the move, but that he was the principal of the school. It was his decision and if he felt moving me from the fourth to the sixth grade was in the best interests of the school, I would go along with it and do my best.

About three weeks later he told me he couldn't find another sixth grade teacher and, since they were going to reshuffle the fourth grade quite a bit because of changes in enrollment, he wanted me to go to the sixth grade. I had no choice but to go.

I told my class on Monday, a week before I was to leave. Some of them took it in right away but others didn't because they were present-oriented and I was still right there in the classroom. They didn't worry about it too much; but some of the brighter ones made remarks such as, "Why can't they get another teacher? Why does it have to you?" One of them said, "Maybe we shouldn't have been such a good class, then they wouldn't take you away."

On Friday there was a good deal of tension in the class, but there wasn't any real resentment. It was kind of an attitude of resignation—that this is the way things are and we can't do anything about it. Life hadn't taught them to expect much, and they just kind of resigned themselves to their fate.

I couldn't do anything either, but I can't say that I was exactly resigned.

My first day in the sixth grade was pretty awkward. First, their former teacher had been in the school for six years and he was an established teacher—a very good teacher with an excellent reputation. They weren't any happier to lose him than my kids had been to have me go. Second, I didn't really get too much help as far as what I was supposed to do and what I was supposed to teach. I had a couple of conferences with the other teacher, but I was just put on my own with the knowledge that these children in my official class, the 6-1 class, had finished the sixth-grade math curriculum and had covered motion, the camera, and electricity in science. I was rather in the dark as to what I was going to teach. I also had another class, the 6-5 section, for science and math. They are the lowest section in the grade and are just starting decimals.

I walked in that first day without exactly knowing what I should be teaching nor how to go about it. We had a short discussion of what I expected of them and how sorry I was to have to replace their very fine teacher. I said that teachers are all different and that I would expect generally the same kind of things he had expected but it might seem a little different at first.

I went over generally what we would learn for the rest of the year—some of the things I had in mind, and then we had a clean up of the room so I could get to know where things were. They pretty well sat and listened to me. I never lost control of the class. I think it is a little more relaxed than it was before, but they came gradually to understand what I expected of them.

Individually the members of this 6-1 class are a fine group of children. They are very verbal, they have experienced a great many things, and you can talk to them on a fine adult level. But when they get together as a whole group, they have no discipline. When one starts talking, they all join in. They show a great lack of respect for one another. If one makes a mistake, they all laugh.

They have had excellent teachers all the way up. In the fifth grade they had a very fine teacher who was even tempered and consistent and, as far as I know, never raised her voice. She had good discipline, knew her curriculum and taught well. But from what I heard, she used to comment in the teachers' room at lunch that she couldn't wait until June to get rid of this class—that they were a very obnoxious bunch of children. All the teachers say that when you have children by themselves they are fun to talk to, but when you get them together as a class they have no kind of discipline. They want everything handed to them rather than working for things themselves. They have an attitude of "show us."

There is also a great deal of competition in the group. I don't know if it is their greater academic potential, their greater awareness of things around them, or their greater sensitivity about things that causes this competition and poor sportsmanship. Rarely did the 4-4 class laugh at each other's mistakes, and the 6-5 class doesn't do it much, either. The 6-1 class does.

They are a very bright group. Four of five girls in the group took the test for a private junior high school for gifted students, and there must have been eleven to fourteen who were nominated for special placement in junior high school. They know this and it makes for a lot of competition.

There is one girl in the class who is a problem. Roma does her work hurriedly and sloppily. She is looked upon by everyone in the class as the most intelligent, even though she gets B's on her math tests. She is the type of student who understands things quickly; she can do all the adding, she understands the process of multiplicaton, but when she starts putting them to work for her she will go quickly, make some silly error and cause the whole problem to be wrong. I was like Roma. I knew how to do the math problems but I was so busy trying to get the answers that I would do something like subtract five from thirteen and get nine—a silly mistake, and yet it was part of the problem.

Our organization in the sixth grade is more a semi-departmentalized type of teaching instead of real team teaching. I teach math and science to the 6-1 and 6-5 groups. I also have my 6-1 group for spelling and some study time, and I have a physical education period with both groups.

The schedule works something like this: First thing in

the morning, I have spelling and individual work with the
6-1 class. About 9 :15, three or four members of the 6-5 group
who are good in math come in to work in the math class with
us. These are Chinese girls who are very good in mathematics but have difficulty with the language. They have been
put in the slower class until they acquire a better command
of English. Two or three of my children go into the 6-5 class
for math. These children have good potential, but they are
underachievers, and a little listless and lethargic toward
school.

This changing back and forth would be easier if the
groups were nearer the same in ability. Last year the highest and the two middle groups worked together with three
teachers. But this year, the two people who were left and
wanted to work together had the highest and the lowest
groups, so that is how it worked out and we do what we can.

At 10:00 the 6-1 group goes to the other teacher for
language arts—writing, penmanship, poetry, whatever the
other teacher is going to do. And her class comes to me for
math. At 10:45 I take this slower group to gym.

My own class comes back into my classroom at 11:00 for
science. At 11:45, the monitors, who are mostly from the
6-1 class, leave to go to their monitorial duties and the last
fifteen minutes is just general discussion and answering
questions and talking. I get to talk with individuals quite a
lot at this time.

In the afternoon I have the 6-5 group in science while
the other teacher teaches social studies to my group. Then
the rest of the time is taken up with released time, assemblies,
and art and music with special teachers. In the spring the
glee club spends a lot of time rehearsing for the Spring
Festival.

I was put into the science without much idea of what
I was supposed to teach. The bulletins are fairly good but
I don't have enough materials to plan a good class for every
day in the week. Therefore, I try to talk a lot with the classes
about basic concepts. When I can get materials together I
have experiments to emphasize and reinforce what I teach.
With the slow group I also try to concentrate on the basic
skills of writing up reports, finding information in reference

books and working together in committees. The other teachers do not allow them to do this kind of thing.

At first I didn't have many books, but I gradually got more. The college gave me some; others I bought at sales or borrowed from libraries. Some of the children became interested enough to bring in books they had gotten their parents to buy for them. So there are enough for everyone.

There is a real difference in what the two groups in science are able to do. One of the areas I teach is about molecules and atoms and the structure of matter. I boiled water to show how the molecules were being heated and moving apart. The slower group got the idea but that is where it stopped. In the other class, they want to know why these things are happening. Were the molecules exploding? What's between the molecules? And they keep asking questions that lead into other sources of knowledge and other areas.

The books I have help to push them along. I enjoy teaching science in the bright group; there isn't as much stimulation in the slower group. I need more materials to make things clearer for them and they're not as curious about things. That may be because they are slower children, or it may be that they have been stifled throughout their school years because they have known only failure and frustration. I think a lot of it is due to lack of materials in the school and lack on the teacher's part in knowing how to handle the children and how to meet their problems. All these things build up and the result is a combination of all these factors. It presses down upon the teacher and unfortunately, it's the child who comes out at the low end of the stick.

The sixth-grade assignment is a tremendous challenge to me, and I like it. I followed a teacher who had been teaching there for four or five years and had a clear idea of what he wanted to do. He knew what his students were capable of and had his discipline already set. The children liked him and respected him. I had to move into this situation and try to teach a lot of things I'm not quite sure I have the background for. It is a challenge but it is a great responsibility.

I think the general idea of the team teaching is good. I think I am gaining a lot from working with the other teacher. She is an excellent teacher. I am learning a great deal from her in terms of curriculum, of handling children, of knowing myself a little bit better. I think she is learning some things from me, too.

It is a fairly good working unit that we have established. We do some planning together but not a great deal. In the morning we usually talk a little bit about what has happened and how the children behaved themselves. This is not really planning, because I am taking one segment of the curriculum and she is taking the other, but we each know pretty well what the other is doing. We do try to correlate our work whenever we can. In social studies, she was working on Latin America, so I showed a film on the Amazon River and talked about the importance of water as it fitted into the work on biology. Our science reports also reinforced the work on writing and speaking that she was doing in language arts.

I think the children benefit from the team teaching situation. I know it allows the teacher more time to go into specific curriculum areas and do better teaching than if he has to cover all areas. Then, too, it gives the children a good taste of what it is like to switch classes, to move back and forth and conduct themselves in a correct way. They learn that there are different teachers who teach in different ways, and for forty-five minutes they have to concentrate on just one subject, such as science or math. I think it is a distinct advantage for pupils who are going to junior high school.

As for allowing a teacher to get to know his students, working with them over a longer period of time, and enjoying himself at the job, this situation is different from the fourth-grade class. I think the 6-5 group needs the same kind of individual work and socialization experiences that my 4-4 group had, but it is hard to do much when I have them only part of the time. I didn't care for the arrangement in the beginning and I still find drawbacks but I think that it is a worthwhile experience for most of the children.

Next year I want to go back to a lower grade, and I want a slow class. I want to find out more about how the younger children learn but primarily I want to see what I can do about the frustration that comes so early to these children. That is what is so saddening about the 6-5 class. They don't want to try anymore. They read on a third- or fourth-grade level. They don't have the ability to use reference books, to look up things for themselves and find out things. I think this should be caught as soon as possible and the earlier the better. I think a third-grade class—a slow one—would be a good place to begin. I will probably not see any results by the fourth grade but I hope they will be further advanced when they get to the sixth grade than the class I have now. I firmly believe that if these children are not helped and their concepts are not developed and their experiences are not broadened in the lower grades, the teacher encounters an almost hopeless battle in the sixth and seventh grades; the children just do not have the skills or the desire to go out and learn things on their own.

I've learned a lot this year but two things stand out. I like to call them my two keys to teaching in depressed-area schools. The first is anticipation of what is going to happen. A great deal of this can be gained through reading, observing other teachers, and just the sheer intellectual process of sitting down and thinking things out. However, a lot can be gained only through being in an actual situation, doing something wrong, realizing what has happened, and knowing that the next time you will anticipate and will not make the same mistake again.

Another thing, besides anticipation, is consistency of thought, of action, and of feeling for the children. In the classroom I always try to exhibit as much respect as possible for each child—concern over sniffles, or a slight cold, complimenting them on a nice, new shirt, or seeing that a certain boy has on new shoes or a girl has a new sweater. It means that as you go around the classroom you show your concern by reaching out and patting a child on the shoulder when you are asking a question or answering a question. You always let him know that you like him no matter what he does or how often you have to discipline him.

It is through anticipation and consistency that I feel a teacher in a depressed area can make the greatest progress in helping these children to learn to live with each other and to respect themselves and other people as much as possible.

6

The teacher's task

Any teacher who is trying to do a reasonably competent job works hard. Teachers in slum schools must generally work harder and expect less tangible results. The failures, difficulties, and frustrations of the four beginning teachers whose experiences have been recounted in this book illustrate the problems. But the account shows, too, the special satisfactions and rewards that come to those who persevere. In a very special sense, the popular expression, "It's a great life if you don't weaken," describes the situation of the teacher in depressed urban areas. This is no place for weakness. Strength of commitment, clarity of purpose and a positive response to challenge is necessary. The comment, "If this gets easy, I wouldn't want to do it," illustrates well the characteristic orientation of the teachers who choose to work in difficult schools.

But in considering his readiness to teach children of the urban slums, the prospective teacher must realize that dedication and commitment, while supremely important, are by no means the only prerequisities. A fine general education which combines breadth of interest and depth of scholarship is basic. A carefully planned program of professional preparation which includes student teaching under the direction of an experienced teacher is also a necessity. But more is needed.

Specialized knowledge of the lives and learning styles of the children of the slums is an important requirement. In some colleges it is now possible for the prospective teacher to take helpful courses in urban sociology and cultural anthropology. Recent studies of the culture of poverty and the characteristics and problems of present-day minority groups can furnish valuable background. Some exploratory discussions of the educational implications of these conditions have been published and provide many useful insights while illustrating clearly the lack of systematic study and conceptualization in the field. Current articles in lay and professional magazines, as well as some autobiographical and fictional materials, are very helpful. A growing knowledge of the literature in the field is an important part of preparation of teachers for urban schools.

Another source of insight is first-hand experience in the schools and other institutions of the depressed urban community. For many teachers whose own backgrounds are limited to comfortable suburban or middle-class urban living, the slum community is essentially unknown. Observation and participation in the schools of the area provide a limited opportunity to learn something of the children and their learning styles. Volunteer work in community agencies and after-school programs offer another dimension. Walking tours of the community and conversations with businessmen, social workers, clergymen, politicians, and police officers will give additional experience. Contacts with parents in organized groups, in conferences at school, in protest meetings, and in home visits are extremely helpful. Also of value are extended interviews with school guidance workers and other school personnel.

Concern for understanding the community and the backgrounds of the pupils in the school is not new. Professional literature is filled with exhortations to teachers to know the school community. In the case of the middle class teacher who is considering work in a depressed area, however, it serves as vital a role as the junior year abroad for the student of French culture.

Such realistic understanding of the conditions which influence the teacher's task may spell the difference between the starry-eyed idealist who goes forth to uplift the masses but retires in bitter defeat after the first week of school and the informed professional who has calculated the odds and knows that he may lose many battles but will find challenge and satisfaction in the continuing struggle.

PLANNING FOR LEARNING

When his preservice preparation is completed, and his decision to work in a depressed-area school confirmed by the acceptance of an assignment to a particular teaching position, the beginning teacher is ready to consider next steps. The most immediate and essential next step is the development of careful plans for promoting desirable learning in his classroom.

To many teachers, the term "lesson plan" connotes a detailed statement of pious hopes developed for the perusal of the college supervisor or school administrator. There is no doubt that entries in the approved schedule books are often made to meet the requirements of the person in authority rather than for the guidance of the teacher in the classroom. It is equally true, however, that no single aspect of the teaching process is more important than the careful, informed planning that the teacher does regularly throughout every working day and week and year. In fact, on the quality of a teacher's planning depends a great deal of his success or, in the case of a beginning teacher, a great part of his chance for survival.

Successful planning depends upon knowledge in a number of areas. The teacher must know his teaching fields, appropriate methods, and instructional skills, but he must also know the children for whose learning he plans.

Information which is helpful in understanding the disadvantaged child is beginning to be available. Identifiable group characteristics appear among the undoubted diversities of individuals. The teacher must plan in terms of these characteristics while broadening his knowledge of each child and his special learning needs.

The immediate consideration with any class is deciding where to start. What do they already know and what are they able to learn at this time? The previous year's achievement tests and school records will give some indication as to what the child has done in the past. While not accepting them as valid predictors of future achievement, the teacher will find such records useful as a basis for planning. There are other factors to be considered, however.

With all but the youngest children, the reading level is probably far below that of the ubiquitous national norms, so widely revered and so little understood. Reading is not an important part of these children's lives. Papers, magazines, and books are rarely found in the home; few adults have the leisure or the ability to read extensively; crowded, noisy apartments do not encourage sustained study and a reading textbook is often viewed as a symbol of frustration and failure.

But school books do not constitute the only avenue to a successful understanding of the printed word. It is interesting to speculate how much more relevant reading might seem if it were taught through television commercials, the lyrics of popular songs or signs in store windows and on subway cars. The beginning teacher might find these sources of printed materials, supplemented by pupil-made books and experience charts, of great value in building a readiness for more formal reading instruction at any level.

In mathematics, too, the number combinations may be difficult to memorize and the textbook problems lacking in meaning but the children of poverty are not unacquainted with numerical relationships and values. Earlier than middle-class children, they handle money, do the family shopping, and buy their own clothes. Practical problems involving the economics of "two for" pricings and various sized containers may be meaningful and valuable in laying a foundation for further development of mathematical skills and understandings. Again, the teacher's plans show his awareness of the experiences and backgrounds of his pupils as well as the requirements of his subject matter.

Social studies books are often difficult to read and far off times and places are little understood. The names of cities and states and countries, including those in which the pupils live, may be hopelessly confused. These children rarely leave the narrow world of the block and then only to plunge beneath the ground and emerge later in the totally disconnected space surrounding the hospital, the Welfare Office, or the public beach. But while spatial relations may be confusing, the children of the block are not unaware of social distinctions and processes. The Negro child knows that beyond the ghetto there is a white world in which he has no part. The dark lad from the Island proudly parrots his mother's assertion that he is Hispanos and no relation to an American ex-slave.

All the children know much of Welfare—the shame of men who cannot find work to feed their families and the tyranny of the black book which controls the minutest circumstances of their lives. They know first-hand birth and death and hunger and violence and neighborly kindness. They may be unimpressed by the pasteboard figures of community helpers that inhabit their social studies books, but they have a clear picture of the status of each person in their crowded world and his usefulness—or danger—to them.

They know, too, much better than middle-class children, how to look after themselves and the younger children who may be dependent on them. A ten-year-old may wear the latch key around his neck, escort his brothers and sisters to and from school, and prepare the evening meal before his mother returns from work. Such relationships are not always harmonious or the methods of control gentle but the younger child can be assured of a devoted champion against any threat from outside the family group.

Yes, these children know many things but it is far from easy to reconcile "the conflicting demands of the two cultures in which they live—the one of the home and the neighborhood, the other of the school and the society that maintans it."[1] In planning for learning the teacher must attempt to build bridges between the two cultures and to help the child attain more meaningful relationships with the world in which he lives.

This often involves new curriculum content and organization adapted to the task at hand. Traditional grade levels have little meaning and usual content is often inappropriate. Imagination and sensitivity are needed to plan meaningful activities for ten-year-olds who have very limited reading

---

[1] Miriam L. Goldberg, "Adapting Teacher Style to Pupil Differences: Teachers for Disadvantaged Children," *Merrill-Palmer Quarterly of Behavior and Development*, 1964, 10(2), p. 168.

skills and a negative attitude toward school. Curriculum bulletins are often of little help, and the usual fifth-grade textbooks are largely unusable. But new materials are becoming available in all areas and help is on the way for the teacher who is prepared to use it intelligently. It is not the topics covered or the pages assigned that define the amount of learning which takes place. It may be that the teacher who "covers" the least may uncover the greatest ability and potential for achievement among his pupils.

As the teacher makes his plans for classroom activities, he will find it helpful to stop every now and then and ask, "Why should the children study the material included in this lesson? What possible meaning can it have?" and "If not this, what then?"

These are not easy questions to answer honestly. Habit and the weight of custom support the obvious cliches: "Everyone should know it," or "It's in the course of study." Further thought may produce quite different answers. Even when the young teacher cannot find the means for making immediate changes in the curriculum content which he perceives to be lacking in value for his group, he will plan his work differently when he has raised and answered the pertinent questions without reservation.

When setting up the sequence of activities throughout the school day, the teacher needs to consider carefully the variety and timing of pupil participation. Even a favorite poem or an exciting story may fail to secure uninterrupted attention if it follows immediately after an assembly program or a long period of concentrated written work. A change in pupil activity is as important as a change in subject matter content. Opportunities to move, to speak, to write, to compete against time, to engage in leisurely thought, must be a part of the school day. The teacher's plans need to provide for a variety of pupil responses and a change of pace as well as for lesson content.

A final aspect of planning is making provision for some evaluation of the results of the projected teaching behavior. Teachers teach that children may learn. What they learn, how much, and with what effort are the bases both for evaluation of results and for future planning. If the teacher knows, as a result of a check at the end of today's lesson, that all but five children can spell all the week's spelling words correctly, he may then plan for a period of special help for those five, but not for further study by the whole group. Provision for assessing the results of teaching activities in terms of pupil behavior produces more effective immediate planning. It is also a significant factor in the difference between the implications of twenty years' teaching experience and one year's experience repeated twenty times.

CLASSROOM ORGANIZATION AND CONTROL

Every beginning teacher worries about discipline. Teachers in depressed area schools often have nightmares. The awful moment when the door closes and the teacher is alone in a room with thirty or more young humans is the culmination of years of preparation. There is but one thought in the minds of most neophyte teachers: "Will the children obey me?" Usually they will—for the first day or two.

It is what happens during those first few days, while the class members are sizing up the new teacher and gathering their forces for the inevitable testing time to come, that decides the fate of many would-be pedagogues. It is then that the stage is set for a year which is characterized by strife and despair or by order and satisfaction.

It is in these first days that a specialized aspect of planning becomes most important. As the director plots the action of his play, the teacher must lay out the routines which will guide the movements of his class. How will the children enter the classroom and be dismissed? When and for what purpose is it permissible for a pupil to leave his seat? What are the procedures for gaining recognition from the teacher, for speaking to classmates, for securing supplies? The seeming insignificance of these repetitive activities is deceiving. If carefully established and continually enforced, they may become merely convenient facilitators of the main business of learning. If left to chance, or the whim of the moment, they may become sources of disorder and irritation throughout the year.

It is easy to say that essential routines must be set during the first week of school, but how are these magic essentials to be identified? So many things seem terribly important when perfection is the goal and chaos an immediate prospect. Gum chewing is a convenient illustration. Everyone knows that children must not chew gum in school. It is relatively simple to state a rule to that effect. But saying will not make it so and the statement commits the teacher to an immediate battle that can be both exhausting and without much prospect of permanent victory. It may be that concern for gum chewing can be postponed until some later date when the problems of paper wrappers, sticky deposits on furniture, and communication impeded by bovine jaw exercises may be reasonably discussed and restrictive covenants agreed upon.

The problem of an effective seating arrangement for the classroom is related closely to the desire for quiet individual work and the prevention of assault and battery. Working out seating arrangements which will effectively isolate the talkers and the troublemakers by surrounding them with the quiet and the conforming is a challenging task on which many young teachers expend considerable energy. Unfortunately, it is an equal challenge to the children to prove that they can create an interesting environment for themselves under adverse circumstances. And here the teacher is badly outnumbered and doomed to almost certain defeat. Except in a few instances where two individuals obviously cannot peaceably continue to occupy adjacent territory, it may be that a better plan is to set up a carefully thought-out permanent seating arrangement and rely on other measures for keeping the noise level to a dull roar and aggression at a minimum.

Routines for entering and leaving the room, for passing through crowded halls, and for securing recognition from the teacher *are* necessary, and here a careful definition of limits and unceasing enforcement is the rule. The slum child especially needs the structure which he often lacks in his out-of-school life. His desk, his books, his coat hook, and his place in line take on exaggerated significance for the child who has so little which is dependably his alone. The defense of his own rights is often coupled with a sporting effort to get what belongs to someone else. Eternal vigilance and good-humored enforcement of clearly established regulations are required. It may seem quite unimportant, at the end of a busy and trying day, who walks in front of whom in line, but the wise teacher will see that all is in order before he starts the long journey down the stairs with scheduled stops for regrouping of forces. Few aspects of the day's work are more frustrating, and he will need all the support that established procedures can give him.

Obviously, communication in the classroom requires a certain degree of quiet. It is only at cocktail parties and similar functions that everyone can talk at the same time and be presumed to be listening as well. However, the teacher will do well to think carefully about the relation between his traditional dream of classroom quiet and the requirements of effective learning and communication. It may be that listening for pins to drop is not always the most productive educational activity.

When the teacher talks, children should listen but this desirable goal will be greatly facilitated if the teacher exercises a reasonable control over his verbal activity. Many slum children have learned effective procedures for tuning out much of the static of their crowded environment. Quarreling, bickering, threatening, complaining, demanding— these are familiar constants in the home—and in self-defense the child learns not to listen. In school, a discursive, nagging teacher meets the same fate. Children either retreat to think their own thoughts or, perhaps more characteristically, find other activities which interest them more. Clear, concise stating of directions and procedures is a skill worthy of the best efforts of the teacher. When clarity is supplemented by enthusiasm and brevity by understanding, communication becomes an art and the development of listening habits becomes progressively less difficult.

If the child is to listen intelligently, however, he must also have opportunities to speak. This is where the ideal of the quiet classroom must be closely scrutinized. Even without the incontestable evidence that teachers talk a great deal, it is evident that when the time allowed for pupil participation is divided by thirty, very little is left for each individual.

Everything known about slum children attests to their need for improved communication in the essentially new language known as standard English. Opportunities to use the school-approved way of speaking, to increase vocabulary, to put thoughts into words, is vitally important and should be a part of the planned activity of every classroom. There may also be some place for just talking.

The decision as to whether a child may speak only when recognized by the teacher or in some other specifically designated situations is an important one. When the decision is made it should be clearly defined and consistently enforced. It is probably no more difficult to build habits of controlled, limited talking than to enforce absolute silence, and there may be greater value in the former.

Suppose, for instance, that children are permitted to talk softly to one another about their schoolwork during periods of independent activity. Such limited communication may be difficult to control at first, but it can bring very worthwhile results in enabling the children to explain assignments, suggest solutions, and help each other in many ways. Maximum learning is the goal, and the teacher may well find the other students to be valuable allies in imparting information and developing skills. The school-related notion of individual work is by no means the only way of promoting effective learning. The man behind the wheel must finally pass the driver's test, but he may have had many teachers and much advice during the learning period.

Group activity provides another means for cooperative learning and for differentiation of instruction. The organizational ability required to plan and control effective group work is considerable. Beginning teachers are often warned of the dangers involved and advised to keep the group together until they are secure in their ability to control the class. Like all general admonitions, this well-meant advice is not infallible. It may well be that the range of ability in the school subjects is so wide that total group instruction is a bore to the best and a mystery to the poorest pupils in the class. The child who never knows his place in the basic reader may be completely absorbed in a trade book on a subject of his own choosing. This disruptive, uncooperative repeater may develop pride in individual achievement when given an opportunity to work with SRA materials at his own reading level.

The teacher will do well, therefore, to weigh the difficulties of divided attention against the potential opportunities for greater learning when deciding whether or not to attempt some grouping of pupils for instruction. In any event, he will be wise to make haste slowly.

The need for differentiated instruction in skill subjects is the most common impetus for grouping pupils in the classroom. Providing special materials for a few individuals who differ markedly from most of the class in reading, for instance, may ease the frustrations of the very capable or the very slow student while presenting little added complexity in the classroom organization. Since the successful and challenged learner is more likely to be a cooperative pupil, such an arrangement can make the teacher's job easier.

As the teacher's ability in stage-managing varied activities increases, it may be possible to set up groups in other skill areas and to begin some simple, cooperative, learning activities which are also types of group work. Again, the initial involvement of a limited number of individuals and a provision for space and needed materials is important. The beginning teacher can use a variety of groupings in his classroom if he plans carefully for each activity and takes time to give explicit directions to his pupils. It takes patience to develop the self-control necessary for effective group work; brief periods of group activity may profitably be alternated with more structured lessons. Self-control is not learned without varied opportunities for practice, however, and it may well be that group work in the classroom provides such opportunities most effectively.

In addition to important decisions about routines and classroom organization, the beginning teacher must also exercise restraint and good judgment in deciding when to solve his discipline problems by himself and when to seek assistance. Excessive dependence on the teacher next door, the grade leader or the principal is both inadvisable and ineffective.

There are times, however, when help is not only desirable but necessary. When a child is threatening the safety of the other members of the group, he must be restrained. If the teacher is physically unable to protect the other children from his aggression, help must be obtained. The long-range solution may be disciplinary action by an administrator, help from the guidance counselor, or more effective handling by the teacher, but the immediate situation requires action by whoever is available.

An emotionally disturbed child should be referred to the guidance counselor, but such a referral needs to be supported by detailed and specific anecdotal records. In this situation, an objective report is worth many emotional accounts of difficulties. Certainly both the child and the teacher will be aided if the guidance counselor has the information he needs to render effective professional assistance. The beginning teacher will find the guidance counselors in his school a ready source of advice and help. He should not hesitate to seek aid when he needs it.

There are some instances when it is very desirable to have a child temporarily removed from the classroom. When all other means have failed, two or three days' relief may enable the teacher to get the rest of the class functioning smoothly. In such a situation the teacher is justified in asking for help, but he must be very sure that he has used all means in his power to work out his class control for himself. The temporary removal solves nothing, but it provides a needed respite and makes possible a fresh start. This is as important for the teacher as it is for the child.

Hopefully, the school principal has the time and the will to give support and counsel to the beginning teacher. As the administrative officer closest to the teacher his influence can be decisive. Even the best-prepared teacher needs a sympathetic ear when things go wrong. Most fortunate is he who finds it.

But there is a limit to what anyone can do to help the beginning teacher. He alone must establish himself in his classroom as the person in charge. Firmly and consistently, he must demonstrate his determination to control the situation. This determination will frequently be challenged and there will be constant temptation to relax temporarily or give up entirely on some point. It takes a stubborn individual to hold his course in the midst of the frustrations of the first weeks of school.

These frustrations are often intensified by the feeling that discipline occupies too much of the teacher's time, that he has no opportunity to share with children the joy and satisfaction of successful learning. At first, this may be true. But the teacher who is firm and consistent soon learns that he does not have to be harsh and aloof. Of course, there are teachers who rule their classrooms through fear. But these teachers do not gain the respect of their children. If discipline is defined as the ability to achieve respect and attention in the classroom, the teacher who rules through fear has achieved only one aspect of discipline. He can force attention, but not respect. The teacher who would have not only respect and attention, but also cooperation and acceptance, must show children that he likes and understands them in spite of their difficulties. He must plan classroom activities which make cooperation seem worthwhile and, above all, he must set up an organized classroom structure which provides the children with a comfortable, secure environment. Such an environment reduces greatly the need for disciplinary action.

This discussion of classroom control may be summarized in a few simple guidelines which are easy to state but far from easy to follow. They should be applied intelligently and modified or adapted as necessary to the specific situation.

1. When establishing basic routines in the classroom, state clearly the reasons for the rules but make it plain to the pupils that obedience is required. You are in charge and your directions must be carried out.
2. Set up only a few rules at first. Consistency of action on your part is extremely important. If a great number of rules are established, it is very hard to enforce them all fairly and consistently.
3. Learn to discriminate between important and unimportant disciplinary situations. Avoid confrontations with a

defiant child in front of the class. Do not allow yourself to be forced into a situation in which you must use punitive measures in order to "save face."

4. Recognize that children are individuals who are worthy of respect. As a teacher, you must have respect for yourself and respect for children. Children like teachers whom they respect; friendship is not promoted by weakness and indecision.

5. Consistently accentuate the positive. By being polite, honest, and fair, you can promote control. Children learn through imitation; they learn courtesy and fairness by your example.

6. Present the children with a model of a well-organized, competent adult. They need someone they can trust, someone they can depend on to be the same day after day.

7. Finally, remember, you are responsible for what goes on in your classroom. If you are convinced of your own authority and power, you have gone a long way toward convincing your pupils.

RESPONSIBILITY FOR PARTICIPATION

A new teacher's major concern is inevitably his own classroom. When that classroom is filled with a large number of young humans whose needs are great and whose reactions are not readily predicted, the concern deepens. The problems of establishing routines, of securing conformity to necessary regulations, of planning lessons and maintaining the interest of the group, of avoiding disruption and loss of that all-important control, seem—and are—enormous. Their immediacy causes any other demands to appear as unrelated annoyances.

But when an individual accepts his first teaching position, he becomes a part of several groups which demand his allegiance and his cooperative efforts. The most important of these are the school staff, the community, and the profession.

A school staff is made up of teachers, administrators, a larger or smaller number of resource persons with specialized functions, and service personnel. In theory, school principals, corrective reading teachers, guidance workers, nurses, and other special personnel are in the school to facilitate the job of the teacher. Often, however, the beginning teacher gains quite the opposite impression of their function. Lesson plans must be written for the principal, the nurse must have the completed health cards today, detailed reading records were due a week ago, and few lessons go uninterrupted by impatient messengers with forms to be completed. All of this is difficult to accept.

In time, it will be possible to anticipate most clerical tasks and plan for them without undue interruption of classroom activities. Eventually their meaning and usefulness might even become clear. But the teacher who would discharge his duties as a staff member and win the approval and gratitude of administrative personnel will make every effort to complete his reports accurately and on time. A school, like any other large enterprise involving many people, must depend on cooperation from all employees. An administrator may be intellectually convinced that there are many things far more important in a new teacher than his ability to keep a register, but on the day the district report is due, and the school clerk has spent half the morning attempting to account for discrepancies in the records, his annoyance may overcome his nicely balanced sense of priority.

It may take some time for the new teacher to discover what services and special help administrators and other resource personnel are willing—and able—to give. It may take even longer to learn to accept gracefully or use effectively those services which are made available. The principal may or may not be an effective aid in establishing authority and dealing with discipline problems. Supervisory visits may be a source of encouragement and stimulation or an ordeal to be endured. Suggestions made and activities proposed may not seem practical at the time. A special teacher may provide an enriched program and a valued experience, or he may leave a demoralized and disorderly class at the end of each visit. And words of approval and approbation for honest effort may be long in arriving or never come at all.

The other teachers, particularly those who have been in the school some time or who teach on the same grade level, can be very helpful. They have much knowledge concerning school expectations, the principal's idiosyncrasies, and the procedures for obtaining supplies. The teacher's lunchroom can be a spot well worth frequenting, both for the therapeutic effect of sharing frustrations and for the practical help that may be gained from the suggestions of others. As time goes on, the novice will undoubtedly be drawn into his own circle of congenial colleagues. At first, a wide acquaintance and a willingness to participate in a variety of activities may prevent a premature choice.

While it is certainly well to consider thoughtfully the words of older and wiser colleagues, wisdom does not necessarily grow with age. Neither is it always helpful to accept without question the attitudes of the teacher next door. Ability to discriminate comes with experience and individual soul-searching. In the meantime, courteous listening costs nothing.

The teacher also has responsibilities to the community in which he teaches. His participation here is difficult both to define and to achieve. The relations of the urban school with the people it serves have never been close. The present situation is one of increased awareness and increased tension.

Typically, contacts between teachers and parents are limited. Teachers do not live in the community. They rise out of the subways each morning and descend to return to their comfortable, middle-class communities each afternoon. Parent conferences bog down in the difficulties of communication, when they are held at all. Usually it is only the mothers of well-behaved children who appear at conference time to ask the traditional question, "Is he good in school?" The others come when sent for by the principal to stand in shame as the offenses of their offspring are recounted. Frustration, anger, and lack of understanding characterize most such confrontations, with language barriers often adding only one more difficulty to the already hopeless situation.

Present conditions make understanding especially difficult for all concerned. Minority groups are aware as never before that inadequate educational opportunities can doom a child to a life of poverty and insecurity. They are being told daily, by mass media, politicians, and local leaders, that the schools are inferior, that their children do not have a chance to achieve. And in parents' associations, in protest meetings, in picketing, and in boycotts, they are demanding better schools, well-prepared teachers, and necessary materials of instruction.

Their concerns are sincere and their demands are warranted. No one can deny the justice of their cause. Equal opportunity for all children, in effective, nonsegregated schools, has long been a stated goal of American society. The distance between the goal and its achievement is the cause of the present discontent. But the new teacher, along with other conscientious professionals, is feeling the frustration and lack of confidence of the community. Children repeat glibly neighborhood comments concerning "bad" schools and "poor" teachers, and all suffer from the undeniable sins of the few.

In this unhappy situation, the new teacher's role must necessarily be a limited one. He must try to understand, to retain his objectivity even under unjustified attack, and to show in all his contacts with parents and other members of the community that he is not indifferent. Attendance at PTA meetings, at open meetings called for discussion of school problems, and at local political gatherings may be helpful and informative. Honest efforts to communicate with parents, to welcome them to the school, to show interest and appreciation, pay big dividends. Home visits, scheduled in advance with parents willing to receive the teacher, can give much-needed insights. Little acts can have great influence. Spending precious weekend hours to take children to museums and parks, remaining after school for an hour to comfort an ill child who must wait for a parent to come from work to take him home, writing notes for children who have shown progress rather than only for those who cause trouble, and stopping to talk with a group of parents outside the school set a teacher apart as one who cares. The condemnation of the school and all its works remains, but Juan's teacher becomes an exception, an individual separate from institutional designations.

It is perhaps through his participation in professional

associations that the teacher has the greatest unrealized opportunity to make his influence felt in his school and his community. Teachers' meetings, educational conferences, and committee assignments are not always the most stimulating or welcome part of a teacher's work. They can, in fact, be deadly. But, like other cooperative enterprises, they depend ultimately upon the convictions and the energy of their members, and few groups are completely hopeless, in spite of first impressions.

The principal may be a frustrated top sergeant and conduct his teachers' meetings like briefings on a military base. More likely, however, he is responding to past experiences with indifferent or antagonistic staff members as he appears before his teachers to deliver repetitive lectures and make routine announcements. It takes time and cooperative effort to secure staff action in many schools, but grade meetings, committee groups, and lunchroom gatherings are always available. The newcomer who volunteers for unwanted assignments may be scorned by disillusioned veterans, but tact, effort, and ingenuity can yield surprising results. Although it is only beginning to be admitted openly, the role of the teacher requires many of the skills and understandings of practical politics. Greater recognition of this fact is important and necessary.

In his participation in formally organized professional organizations, the new teacher is well advised to inform himself thoroughly concerning the program and purposes of the existing groups and to choose his affiliation with care. The teaching profession has far to go in developing effective professional organizations and standards. In a particular situation, one organization may offer greater opportunities for productive action than another. The important responsibility of the new teacher is to choose an organization which he can support, give it as much time and energy as he can, and—humbly, but insistently—make his influence felt in the formulation of policies and action programs which exemplify his beliefs and hopes for the profession.

It is an ambitious program of participation that is outlined here. In the school, the community, and the profession, the teacher's responsibilities are heavy. At times they seem to present an impossible load. But to the resolute, the impossible takes only a little longer, and each step becomes more possible than the last.

THE IMAGE OF THE TEACHER

The teacher represents many things to the slum child. At best, he may provide acceptance, support, and heightened aspiration. At worst, he contributes further evidence of the unconcern, rejection, and inadequacy that are so characteristic of other aspects of the child's life. At all times, however, the teacher is to the child and the community the image of an educated person. In a very special sense the teacher in the slum school symbolizes the effects of the schooling he is engaged in providing for his pupils.

Appearance is one important aspect of this image. Good grooming is as necessary in the classroom as in the office, and appropriate attire is desirable anywhere. Children are very conscious of their teacher's clothing; they respond to variety and color. A crisp, white blouse or a fresh shirt on assembly day sets an example more effective than repeated reminders of the mandated attire. The teacher who cares about his appearance in the classroom encourages personal pride in his students. He is a model to which all may aspire.

In other personal characteristics, too, the child is influenced by the example of his teachers. Standard English is caught as often as it is taught, and increased richness and variety of oral expression come most easily when the teacher's speech exemplifies these qualities. Not only the structure of the teacher's language, but the tone of his speech is catching. A firm, low-pitched voice often results in moderately stated replies; conversely, the teacher who shouts is almost certain to be shouted at.

As an educated person, the teacher may be expected to be an impractical bookworm or a repository of all existing information, but the picture can be broadened to include more important characteristics. The teacher exhibits many intellectual interests in his teaching. He reads and he talks about some of the books he enjoys. He reflects his interest in humanitarian and social causes through visible action and verbal support. He shares with children at appropriate levels his enjoyment of art, music, poetry, or dramatics. He is enthusiastic about learning.

The teacher brings to his professional task all that he is and does. But he must have something to bring. An occupational hazard for the beginning teacher especially is that his demanding job may drain him of all desire or capacity for continued intellectual and personal development.

There is always so much to be done. After correcting papers and planning lessons until late at night, the teacher arrives at school the next day too tired and irritable to teach effectively. Hard work is required and many hours of preparation are needed, but perspective and objectivity are equally important. An evening at a new play is preferable to a sleepless night worrying over petty annoyances. A weekend excursion with friends can bring fresh vision to a problem which has refused to yield to concentrated attention. For teachers, too, a change of pace is important.

Many beginning teachers are not comfortable with the idea of being a model of desired behavior. Still feeling their way into their new role, they find the center of the stage at once too demanding and too revealing. It is well to remember that humanity is more important than perfection and that children who live day-by-day with a teacher in a classroom have ample opportunity to react to continued performance rather than a single unfortunate incident. The teacher can make many mistakes without penalty if he honestly likes and respects the children he teaches. If he lacks these qualities, no repertoire of approved practices will make him a successful teacher.

What, then, does it take to teach effectively in a slum school? It takes dedication and compassion and balance and determination and organization and intestinal fortitude. It involves a willingness to work hard for results that are long in coming. It takes the total resources of a learning, growing, developing human being.

Background readings for beginning teachers

Bloom, Benjamin S., Allison Davis, and Robert Hess. *Compensatory Education for Cultural Deprivation*. New York: Holt, Rinehart, and Winston, 1965.

Board of Education of the City of New York. *The Negro in American History: A Bulletin for Teachers*. New York: The Board, 1964.

Board of Education of the City of New York. *Puerto Rican Profiles*. New York: The Board, 1964.

Crosby, Muriel (Ed.) *Reading Ladders for Human Relations*, 4th Ed. Washington, D. C.: American Council on Education, 1963.

Gittler, Joseph B. (Ed.) *Understanding Minority Groups*. New York: John Wiley and Sons (Science Editions), 1964.

Glazer, Nathan, and Daniel Patrick Mojnhan. *Beyond the Melting Pot: The Negroes, Puerto Ricans, Jews, Italians, and Irish in New York City*. Cambridge, Mass.: Massachusetts Institute of Technology Press and Harvard University Press, 1963.

Goldberg, Miriam L. "Adapting Teacher Styles to Pupil Differences: Teachers for Disadvantaged Children," *Merrill-Palmer Quarterly of Behavior and Development*, 1964, 10, (2), 161–178.

Goodman, Mary Ellen. *Race Awareness in Young Children*, rev. ed. New York: Collier Books, 1964.

Handlin, Oscar. *The Newcomers: Negroes and Puerto Ricans in a Changing Metropolis*. Cambridge, Mass.: Harvard University Press, 1959.

Harrington, Michael. *The Other America.* New York: Macmillan, 1962.

Padilla, Elena. *Up From Puerto Rico.* New York: Columbia University Press, 1958.

Passow, A. Harry (Ed.) *Education in Depressed Areas.* New York: Teachers College Press, Teachers College, Columbia University, 1963.

Riessman, Frank. *The Culturally Deprived Child.* New York: Harper and Brothers, 1962.

Roth, Henry. *Call It Sleep.* New York: Avon Library, 1964.

Silberman, Charles E. *Crisis in Black and White.* New York: Random House, 1964.

Wakefield, Dan. *Island in the City.* Boston: Houghton Mifflin, 1959.